# A cheerful heart has a continual feast.

—

*Proverbs 15:15 HCSB*

# Walking with GOD while Cooking for my Family

*Recipes and Spirit-Lifting Devotions*

Freeman-Smith, a division of Worthy Media, Inc.
134 Franklin Road, Suite 200, Brentwood, Tennessee 37027

*The quoted ideas expressed in this book (but not Scripture verses) are not, in all cases, exact quotations, as some have been edited for clarity and brevity. In all cases, the author has attempted to maintain the speaker's original intent. In some cases, quoted material for this book was obtained from secondary sources, primarily print media. While every effort was made to ensure the accuracy of these sources, the accuracy cannot be guaranteed. For additions, deletions, corrections, or clarifications in future editions of this text, please write Freeman-Smith.*

The Holman Christian Standard Bible™ (HCSB) Copyright © 1999, 2000, 2001 by Holman Bible Publishers. Used by permission.

The Holy Bible, New King James Version (NKJV) Copyright © 1982 by Thomas Nelson, Inc. Used by permission.

The Holy Bible, New International Version®. (NIV) Copyright © 1973, 1978, 1984 International Bible Society. Used by permission of Zondervan. All rights reserved.

Cover Design by Scott Williams/ Richmond & Williams
Page Layout by Bart Dawson

ISBN 978-1-60587-450-0

*Printed in the United States of America*

# Walking with GOD while Cooking for my Family

*Recipes and Spirit-Lifting Devotions*

# Table of Contents

# Introduction

I f you're a woman who has spent more than her fair share of time in the kitchen, you know that cooking can be a joyful experience. When you've planned one of your favorite meals, when you've already found every ingredient in the pantry, when all the recipes deliver as promised, and when your family and friends genuinely enjoy the results, you feel that sense of satisfaction that accompanies a job well done. But sometimes, especially when you're busy, tired, or stressed, the "joy" of cooking may seem to be little more than a distant promise. Thankfully, God stands ready to solve every one of your problems—inside the kitchen and out—if only you decide to walk with Him. Even on those days when the cookies crumble and the brownies burn, your kitchen can be a joyful place if you make certain that God is a full partner in every aspect of your work.

This book is, first and foremost, a celebration of God's love and God's Son. But the book is also a celebration of the kitchen. So if you're one of those women who celebrates good food (not to mention good company), try this experiment: During the next 30 days, read a chapter from this book each morning. If you're already committed to a daily time of worship, this text will enhance that experience. If you are not, the simple act of giving God a few minutes each day will change the tone and direction of your life.

On the pages that follow, you'll find tasty recipes, a heaping helping of timely tips, and a cornucopia of great ideas from noted Christian women. And, of course, you'll also find a treasury of inspired wisdom from God's Holy Word.

Are you willing to allow God to work in you and through you? Are you willing to establish a life-altering relationship with your Creator? And do you desire the eternal abundance and peace that can be yours through God's Son? If so, ask for God's guidance many times each day . . . starting with a regular daily devotional. When you do, you will soon discover that your heavenly Father is not just near, He is here. He's with you in the kitchen and everywhere else, for that matter. And He stands ready, willing, and able to transform you into a new creation—all you must do is walk with Him.

# Chapter 1

# Walking with God, Cooking for Your Family

*Choose for yourselves today the one you will worship . . . .
As for me and my family, we will worship the Lord.*
Joshua 24:15 HCSB

### Today's Big Idea

Your family is a precious gift from above,
a gift that should be treasured,
nurtured, and loved.

You're in the kitchen preparing a meal, and there's nobody else around. But you're not alone. Why? Because God is there, too, and He wants to be a full partner in all of your endeavors, which includes, of course, the time you invest caring for your family.

As every woman knows, family life is a mixture of conversations, mediations, irritations, deliberations, commiserations, frustrations, negotiations and celebrations. In other words, the job of caring for your family is both demanding and varied.

Certainly, in the life of every family, there are moments of frustration and disappointment. Lots of them. But, for those who are lucky enough to live in the presence of a close-knit, caring clan, the rewards far outweigh the frustrations.

Even when the demands of everyday life are great, you must never forget that, if you're a parent or grandparent, you are entrusted with a profound responsibility: nurturing the spiritual growth of your family. Parenting, of course, is a job like no other: at times joyous, at times exhausting. You give your family love, support, help, advice, and cooperation—for starters. You may also serve as the family's manager, banker, arbitrator, housekeeper, babysitter, cook, counselor, medic, and chauffeur. Whew! It's a big job, but with God's help, you're up to the task.

When you walk with God—when you worship Him, praise Him, trust Him, and love Him—He will most certainly bless you and yours in ways that you could have scarcely imagined. So the next time you find yourself alone in the kitchen, remember that you're never really alone. God is always present, and His love endures forever. Because He first loved you, you are now free to share His love and His Good News that little band of men, women, children and babies who gather around your kitchen table. So with no further ado, let your service—and your servings—begin.

## A Timely Tip

Put God first in every aspect of your life. And while you're at it, put Him first in every aspect of your family's life, too.

## *More Ideas about Your Family*

There is so much compassion and understanding that is gained when we've experienced God's grace firsthand within our own families.

Lisa Whelchel

The miraculous thing about being a family is that in the last analysis, we are each dependent of one another and God, woven together by mercy given and mercy received.

Barbara Johnson

A home is a place where we find direction.

Gigi Graham Tchividjian

Living life with a consistent spiritual walk deeply influences those we love most.

Vonette Bright

A man ought to live so that everybody knows he is a Christian, and most of all, his family ought to know.

D. L. Moody

## *More from God's Word*

*Now if anyone does not provide for his own relatives, and especially for his household, he has denied the faith and is worse than an unbeliever.*

1 Timothy 5:8 HCSB

*Love must be without hypocrisy. Detest evil; cling to what is good. Show family affection to one another with brotherly love. Outdo one another in showing honor.*

Romans 12:9-10 HCSB

*If a kingdom is divided against itself, that kingdom cannot stand. If a house is divided against itself, that house cannot stand.*

Mark 3:24-25 HCSB

*Let them first learn to show piety at home and to repay their parents; for this is good and acceptable before God.*

1 Timothy 5:4 NKJV

*Every kingdom divided against itself will be ruined, and every city or household divided against itself will not stand.*

Matthew 12:25 NIV

## A Prayer

*Dear Lord, You have blessed me with a family to love and to care for. Protect my family, Lord. And, let me show them love and acceptance, so that through me they might come to know You. Amen*

## Key Lime Pie

1 prepared 9-inch Graham-cracker crust pie shell
1 can (14 oz.) sweetened condensed milk
3 eggs                              ½ cup fresh key lime juice
½ cup caster sugar for meringue topping

Separate egg whites from egg yolks. Make sure there is no trace of yolk in the whites! Begin by beating the sweetened condensed milk, lime juice and egg yolks in a small mixer bowl. Pour the mixture into the baked pie shell. Bake at 350°F for 8 minutes. While baking filling, beat eggs whites in a large, clean mixer bowl on high speed until soft peaks form, then add sugar gradually until meringue forms hard peaks. Spoon the meringue over the top of the hot pie and use a spoon to form peaks. Bake at 350°F for 10-15 minutes, or until meringue begins to brown.

# Chapter 2

# Recipes for Life

*I urge you now to live the life
to which God called you.*
Ephesians 4:1 NKJV

### Today's Big Idea

Your life is a priceless opportunity,
a gift of incalculable worth.
You should thank God for the gift of life . . .
and you should use that gift wisely.

L ife—inside the kitchen or out—is a glorious gift from God. Treat it that way.

This day, like every other, is filled to the brim with opportunities, challenges, and choices. But, no choice that you make is more important than the choice you make concerning God. Today, as you care for your family and friends, you will either place Him at the center of your plans—or not—and the consequences of that choice have implications that are both temporal and eternal.

Sometimes, we don't intentionally neglect God; we simply allow ourselves to become overwhelmed with the demands of everyday life. And then, without our even realizing it, we gradually drift away from the One we need most. Thankfully, God never drifts away from us. He remains always present, always steadfast, always loving.

As you begin this day, place God and His Son where they belong: in your head, in your prayers, on your lips, and in your heart. And then, with God as your guide and companion, let the journey begin . . .

## A Timely Tip

Life is a wonderful gift from God. Don't forget to thank the Giver.

## *More Ideas about Life*

You have a glorious future in Christ! Live every moment in His power and love.

Vonette Bright

As I contemplate all the sacrifices required in order to live a life that is totally focused on Jesus Christ and His eternal kingdom, the joy seeps out of my heart onto my face in a smile of deep satisfaction.

Anne Graham Lotz

Your life is not a boring stretch of highway. It's a straight line to heaven. And just look at the fields ripening along the way. Look at the tenacity and endurance. Look at the grains of righteousness. You'll have quite a crop at harvest…so don't give up!

Joni Eareckson Tada

The value of a life can only be estimated by its relationship to God.

Oswald Chambers

Like a shadow declining swiftly . . . away . . . like the dew of the morning gone with the heat of the day; like the wind in the treetops, like a wave of the sea, so are our lives on earth when seen in light of eternity.

Ruth Bell Graham

Jesus wants Life for us, Life with a capital L.

John Eldredge

The world has never been stable. Jesus Himself was born into the cruelest and most unstable of worlds. No, we have babies and keep trusting and living because the Resurrection is true! The Resurrection was not just a one-time event in history; it is a principle built into the very fabric of our beings, a fact reverberating from every cell of creation: Life wins! Life wins!

Gloria Gaither

We are common earthenware jars, filled with the treasure of the riches of God. The jar is not important—the treasure is everything.

Corrie ten Boom

## *More from God's Word*

*Shout triumphantly to the Lord, all the earth. Serve the Lord with gladness; come before Him with joyful songs.*

Psalm 100:1-2 HCSB

*Rejoice in the Lord always. Again I will say, rejoice!*

Philippians 4:4 NKJV

*Jesus told him, "I am the way, the truth, and the life. No one comes to the Father except through Me."*

John 14:6 HCSB

*I have set before you life and death, blessing and curse. Choose life so that you and your descendants may live, love the Lord your God, obey Him, and remain faithful to Him. For He is your life, and He will prolong your life in the land the Lord swore to give to your fathers Abraham, Isaac, and Jacob.*

Deuteronomy 30:19-20 HCSB

*He who follows righteousness and mercy finds life, righteousness and honor.*

Proverbs 21:21 NKJV

## A Prayer

*Dear Lord, You have created this glorious universe, and You have created me. Let me live my life to the fullest, and let me use my life for Your glory, today and every day. Amen*

## Unforgettable Peanut Butter Fudge

1 cup milk (or slightly more, but not soupy)
3 cups sugar                           1 cup of peanut butter
½ stick of butter                      1 teaspoon vanilla
1 pinch of salt

Mix sugar, milk, butter, and salt in saucepan. Bring mixture to a boil and stir frequently until the mixture forms a small soft ball when dropped in a cup of water (don't overcook; the ball should be soft, not hard). Remove from stove and add peanut butter and vanilla. Beat mixture until creamy and pour into a greased 9-inch pan. Allow fudge to cool before cutting.

# Chapter 3

# Serving Your Family, Serving God

*The greatest among you will be your servant.*
*Whoever exalts himself will be humbled,*
*and whoever humbles himself will be exalted.*

Matthew 23:11-12 HCSB

## Today's Big Idea

Whether you realize it or not,
God has called you to a life of service.
Your job is to find a place to serve and to get busy.

I f you genuinely seek to discover God's unfolding purpose for your life, you must ask yourself this question: "How does God want me to serve my family and my community today?"

Whatever your path, whatever your career, whatever your calling, you may be certain of this: service to others is an integral part of God's plan for you. Every single day of your life, including this one, God will give you opportunities to serve Him by serving His children. Whether you're in the kitchen, at the workplace, or anyplace in between, please welcome those opportunities with open arms. They are God's gift to you, His way of allowing you to achieve greatness in His kingdom. And of this you can be certain: God wants you to serve early and often, and He will surely reward you for your willingness to share your talents and your time with your family and the world.

## A Timely Tip

Remember the people who live under your roof: Service, like love, should begin at home and work its way out from there.

## *More Ideas about Service*

God wants us to serve Him with a willing spirit, one that would choose no other way.

Beth Moore

No life can surpass that of a man who quietly continues to serve God in the place where providence has placed him.

C. H. Spurgeon

In the very place where God has put us, whatever its limitations, whatever kind of work it may be, we may indeed serve the Lord Christ.

Elisabeth Elliot

Through our service to others, God wants to influence our world for Him.

Vonette Bright

Service is the pathway to real significance.

Rick Warren

Christianity, in its purest form, is nothing more than seeing Jesus. Christian service, in its purest form, is nothing more than imitating him who we see. To see his Majesty and to imitate him: that is the sum of Christianity.

Max Lucado

So many times we say that we can't serve God because we aren't whatever is needed. We're not talented enough or smart enough or whatever. But if you are in covenant with Jesus Christ, He is responsible for covering your weaknesses, for being your strength. He will give you His abilities for your disabilities!

Kay Arthur

If you want to discover your spiritual gifts, start obeying God. As you serve Him, you will find that He has given you the gifts that are necessary to follow through in obedience.

Anne Graham Lotz

## *More from God's Word*

*Worship the Lord your God and . . . serve Him only.*

Matthew 4:10 HCSB

*A person should consider us in this way: as servants of Christ and managers of God's mysteries. In this regard, it is expected of managers that each one be found faithful.*

1 Corinthians 4:1-2 HCSB

*If they serve Him obediently, they will end their days in prosperity and their years in happiness.*

Job 36:11 HCSB

*We must do the works of Him who sent Me while it is day. Night is coming when no one can work.*

John 9:4 HCSB

*Serve the Lord with gladness.*

Psalm 100:2 HCSB

## *A Prayer*

*Dear Lord, when Jesus humbled Himself and became a servant, He also became an example for me. Make me a faithful steward of my gifts, and let me be a humble servant to my loved ones, to my friends, and to those in need. Amen*

## Comfort-Food Meatloaf

1 ½ pounds lean ground beef

1 tablespoon vegetable oil

½ cup chopped onion

1 tablespoon Worcestershire sauce

¾ cup oats (either quick or old-fashioned)

3 tablespoons water (as needed)

¼ cup ketchup

1 ½ teaspoon salt

1 large egg, beaten

Using a large skillet, heat oil (over medium heat) and add chopped onion; cook onion until tender. Then, in a separate bowl, mix all other ingredients with the grilled onions. Shape the mixture into a loaf. Bake in a 13x9-inch pan at 375° for 1 hour, or until done. Use 2 spatulas to remove the cooked meatloaf from pan.

# Chapter 4

# Worshipping Him Everywhere (Yes, Even in the Kitchen)

*Worship the Lord your God and . . . serve Him only.*
Matthew 4:10 HCSB

## Today's Big Idea

When you worship God with a sincere heart,
He will guide your steps and bless your life.

Providing for a family requires work, and lots of it. And whether or not your work carries you outside the home, your good works have earned the gratitude of your loved ones and the praise of your Heavenly Father.

It has been said that there are no shortcuts to any place worth going. Wise women agree. Making the grade in today's competitive workplace is not easy. In fact, it can be very difficult indeed. The same can be said for the important work that occurs within the four walls of your home.

God did not create you and your family for lives of mediocrity; He created you for far greater things. Accomplishing God's work is seldom easy. What's required is determination, persistence, patience, and discipline—which is perfectly fine with God. After all, He knows that you're up to the task, and He has big plans for all of you. Very big plans . . .

## A Timely Tip

Worship reminds you of the awesome power of God. So worship Him daily, and allow Him to work through you every day of the week (not just on Sundays).

## *More Ideas about Your Work*

Ordinary work, which is what most of us do most of the time, is ordained by God every bit as much as is the extraordinary.

Elisabeth Elliot

I seem to have been led, little by little, toward my work; and I believe that the same fact will appear in the life of anyone who will cultivate such powers as God has given him and then go on, bravely, quietly, but persistently, doing such work as comes to his hands.

Fanny Crosby

Spiritual worship is focusing all we are on all He is.

Beth Moore

Wouldn't it make astounding difference, not only in the quality of the work we do, but also in the satisfaction, even our joy, if we recognized God's gracious gift in every single task?

Elisabeth Elliot

God does not want us to work for Him, nor does He want to be our helper. Rather, He wants to do His work in and through us.

Vonette Bright

It's the definition of worship: A hungry heart finding the Father's feast. A searching soul finding the Father's face. A wandering pilgrim spotting the Father's house. Finding God. Finding God seeking us. This is worship. This is a worshiper.

Max Lucado

In Biblical worship you do not find the repetition of a phrase; instead, you find the worshipers rehearsing the character of God and His ways, reminding Him of His faithfulness and His wonderful promises.

Kay Arthur

I am of the opinion that we should not be concerned about working for God until we have learned the meaning and delight of worshipping Him.

A. W. Tozer

## *More from God's Word*

*But an hour is coming, and is now here, when the true worshipers will worship the Father in spirit and truth. Yes, the Father wants such people to worship Him. God is Spirit, and those who worship Him must worship in spirit and truth.*

John 4:23-24 HCSB

*If anyone is thirsty, he should come to Me and drink!*

John 7:37 HCSB

*So that at the name of Jesus every knee should bow—of those who are in heaven and on earth and under the earth—and every tongue should confess that Jesus Christ is Lord, to the glory of God the Father.*

Philippians 2:10-11 HCSB

*And every day they devoted themselves to meeting together in the temple complex, and broke bread from house to house. They ate their food with gladness and simplicity of heart, praising God and having favor with all the people. And every day the Lord added those being saved to them.*

Acts 2:46-47 HCSB

## A Prayer

*Heavenly Father, let today and every day be a time of worship. Let me worship You, not only with words and deeds, but also with my heart. In the quiet moments of the day, let me praise You and thank You for creating me, loving me, guiding me, and saving me. Amen*

## Quick and Tasty Green Bean Casserole

2 large cans of French-cut green beans
1 teaspoon Worcestershire sauce
2 cans cream of mushroom soup
8 ounces of grated cheddar cheese
1 small can of sliced mushrooms
1 can French fried onions

Combine all ingredients (except cheese and onions). Place in casserole dish. Top with cheese and bake in 350° oven for 20 minutes. Top with onions and then bake 10 more minutes.

# Chapter 5

# Positive Thinking, Positive Cooking

*Let us hold on to the confession of our hope
without wavering, for He who promised is faithful.*

Hebrews 10:23 HCSB

## Today's Big Idea

As a Christian, you have every reason
to be optimistic about your future
here on earth and your future in heaven.

The self-fulfilling prophecy is alive, well, and living at your house . . . and in your kitchen. If you trust God and have faith in your abilities, your optimistic beliefs will give you direction and motivation. That's one reason that you should never lose hope, but certainly not the only reason. The primary reason that you, as a believer, should never lose hope, is because of God's unfailing promises.

Make no mistake about it: thoughts are powerful things—your thoughts have the power to lift you up or to hold you down. When you acquire the habit of hopeful thinking, you will have acquired a powerful tool for improving your life. So if you find yourself falling into the spiritual traps of worry and discouragement, seek the healing touch of Jesus and the encouraging words of fellow Christians. And if you fall into the terrible habit of negative thinking, think again. After all, God's Word teaches us that Christ can overcome every difficulty (John 16:33). When God makes a promise, He keeps it.

## A Timely Tip

Focus on possibilities, not stumbling blocks. You may encounter occasional disappointments, and, from time to time, you will encounter failure. But, don't invest large quantities of your life focusing on past misfortunes. Instead, look to the future with optimism and hope . . . and encourage your family members to do the same.

## *More Ideas about Optimism*

It never hurts your eyesight to look on the bright side of things.

Barbara Johnson

The game was to just find something about everything to be glad about—no matter what it was. You see, when you're hunting for the glad things, you sort of forget the other kind.

Eleanor H. Porter

Make the least of all that goes and the most of all that comes. Don't regret what is past. Cherish what you have. Look forward to all that is to come. And most important of all, rely moment by moment on Jesus Christ.

Gigi Graham Tchividjian

We may run, walk, stumble, drive, or fly, but let us never lose sight of the reason for the journey, or miss a chance to see a rainbow on the way.

Gloria Gaither

Dark as my path may seem to others, I carry a magic light in my heart. Faith, the spiritual strong searchlight, illumines the way, and although sinister doubts lurk in the shadow, I walk unafraid toward the enchanted wood where the foliage is always green, where joy abides, where nightingales nest and sing, and where life and death are one in the presence of the Lord.

Helen Keller

If you can't tell whether your glass is half-empty or half-full, you don't need another glass; what you need is better eyesight . . . and a more thankful heart.

Marie T. Freeman

Gratitude unlocks the fullness of life. It turns what we have into enough, and more. It turns denial into acceptance, chaos to order, confusion to clarity. It can turn a meal into a feast, a house into a home, a stranger into a friend. Gratitude makes sense of our past, brings peace for today, and creates a vision for tomorrow.

Melody Beattie

When you affirm big, believe big, and pray big, big things happen.

Norman Vincent Peale

## *More from God's Word*

But if we look forward to something we don't have yet, we must wait patiently and confidently.

Romans 8:25 NLT

Make me hear joy and gladness.

Psalm 51:8 NKJV

My cup runs over. Surely goodness and mercy shall follow me all the days of my life; and I will dwell in the house of the Lord forever.

Psalm 23:5-6 NKJV

I can do everything through him that gives me strength.

Philippians 4:13 NIV

For God has not given us a spirit of fear, but of power and of love and of a sound mind.

2 Timothy 1:7 NLT

## A Prayer

*Lord, let me be an expectant Christian. Let me expect the best from You, and let me look for the best in others. If I become discouraged, Father, turn my thoughts and my prayers to You. Let me trust You, Lord, to direct my life. And, let me share my faith and optimism with others, today and every day that I live. Amen*

## Chunky Guacamole

2 ripe avocados
1 tablespoon lemon juice
1 medium tomato chopped
Diced green chiles

2 tablespoons soy sauce
1 large garlic clove (pressed)
¼ teaspoon red pepper
2 tablespoons chopped onions

Mash avocados with lemon juice. Then stir remaining ingredients into mixture and refrigerate until cool. Serve with tortilla chips.

# Chapter 6

# Finding (and Sharing) Wisdom

*Wisdom is the principal thing; therefore get wisdom.*
*And in all your getting, get understanding.*

Proverbs 4:7 NKJV

## Today's Big Idea

God makes His wisdom available to you.
Your job is to acknowledge, to understand,
and (above all) to use that wisdom.

Where will you find wisdom today? Will you seek it from God or from the world? As a thoughtful woman living in a society that is filled with temptations and distractions, you know that the world's brand of "wisdom" is everywhere . . . and it is dangerous. You live in a world where it's all too easy to stray far from the ultimate source of wisdom: God's Holy Word.

When you commit yourself to daily study of God's Word—and when you live according to His commandments—you will become wise . . . in time. But don't expect to open your Bible today and be wise tomorrow. Wisdom is not like a mushroom; it does not spring up overnight. It is, instead, like a majestic oak tree that starts as a tiny acorn, grows into a sapling, and eventually reaches up to the sky, tall and strong.

Today and every day, as a way of understanding God's plan for your life, you should study His Word and live by it. When you do, you will accumulate a storehouse of wisdom that will enrich your own life and the lives of your family members, your friends, and the world.

## A Timely Tip

If you'd like to become a little wiser, the place to start is with God. And His wisdom isn't very hard to find; it's right there on the pages of the Book He wrote.

## *More Ideas about Wisdom*

If we neglect the Bible, we cannot expect to benefit from the wisdom and direction that result from knowing God's Word.

Vonette Bright

Wisdom is knowledge applied. Head knowledge is useless on the battlefield. Knowledge stamped on the heart makes one wise.

Beth Moore

Knowledge can be found in books or in school. Wisdom, on the other hand, starts with God . . . and ends there.

Marie T. Freeman

Having a doctrine pass before the mind is not what the Bible means by knowing the truth. It's only when it reaches down deep into the heart that the truth begins to set us free, just as a key must penetrate a lock to turn it, or as rainfall must saturate the earth down to the roots in order for your garden to grow.

John Eldredge

The fruit of wisdom is Christlikeness, peace, humility, and love. And, the root of it is faith in Christ as the manifested wisdom of God.

J. I. Packer

When you and I are related to Jesus Christ, our strength and wisdom and peace and joy and love and hope may run out, but His life rushes in to keep us filled to the brim. We are showered with blessings, not because of anything we have or have not done, but simply because of Him.

Anne Graham Lotz

Most of us go through life praying a little, planning a little, jockeying for position, hoping but never being quite certain of anything, and always secretly afraid that we will miss the way. This is a tragic waste of truth and never gives rest to the heart. There is a better way. It is to repudiate our own wisdom and take instead the infinite wisdom of God.

A. W. Tozer

Knowledge is horizontal. Wisdom is vertical; it comes down from above.

Billy Graham

## *More from God's Word*

*For now we see in a mirror, dimly, but then face to face. Now I know in part, but then I shall know just as I also am known.*

1 Corinthians 13:12 NKJV

*But from Him you are in Christ Jesus, who for us became wisdom from God, as well as righteousness, sanctification, and redemption.*

1 Corinthians 1:30 HCSB

*Let the word of Christ dwell in you richly in all wisdom, teaching and admonishing one another in psalms and hymns and spiritual songs, singing with grace in your hearts to the Lord.*

Colossians 3:16 NKJV

*Those who are wise shall shine like the brightness of the firmament, and those who turn many to righteousness like the stars forever and ever.*

Daniel 12:3 NKJV

## A Prayer

*Dear Lord, when I trust in the wisdom of the world, I am often led astray, but when I trust in Your wisdom, I build my life upon a firm foundation. Today and every day I will trust Your Word and follow it, knowing that the ultimate wisdom is Your wisdom and the ultimate truth is Your truth. Amen*

## Old-Fashioned Creamy Chess Pie

5 eggs (beaten)
1 cup granulated sugar
½ cup of cream
1 tablespoon cider vinegar

½ cup melted butter
½ cup light brown sugar
1 teaspoon vanilla extract
1 9-inch unbaked pie shell

Combine granulated and brown sugar. Add eggs. Stir in cream, vinegar, vanilla, and butter. Pour mixture into pie shell. Bake on middle rack at 400° for 10 minutes; then lower temperature to 325° and bake for another 35 to 40 minutes or until gently brown.

# Chapter 7

# Praying Together

*Don't worry about anything, but in everything,
through prayer and petition with thanksgiving,
let your requests be made known to God.*

Philippians 4:6 HCSB

## Today's Big Idea

There's no corner of your life
that's too unimportant to pray about,
so pray about everything.

Does your family pray together often, or just at church? Are you and your friends a little band of prayer warriors, or have you retreated from God's battlefield? Do you and yours pray only at mealtimes, or do you pray much more often than that? The answers to these questions will determine, to a surprising extent, the level of your spiritual health.

Jesus made it clear to His disciples: they should pray always. And so should you. Genuine, heartfelt prayer changes things and it changes you. When you lift your heart to the Father, you open yourself to a never-ending source of divine wisdom and infinite love.

Your family's prayers are powerful. So, as you go about your daily activities in the kitchen or outside it, remember God's instructions: "Rejoice always! Pray constantly. Give thanks in everything, for this is God's will for you in Christ Jesus" (1 Thessalonians 5:16-18 HCSB). Start praying in the morning and keep praying until you fall off to sleep at night. And rest assured: God is always listening, and He always wants to hear from you and yours.

## A Timely Tip

When you've got a choice to make, pray about it—one way to make sure that your heart is in tune with God is to pray often. The more you talk to God, the more He will talk to you.

## *More Ideas about Prayer*

What God gives in answer to our prayers will always be the thing we most urgently need, and it will always be sufficient.

Elisabeth Elliot

Your family and friends need your prayers and you need theirs. And God wants to hear those prayers. So what are you waiting for?

Marie T. Freeman

God says we don't need to be anxious about anything; we just need to pray about everything.

Stormie Omartian

The center of power is not to be found in summit meetings or in peace conferences. It is not in Peking or Washington or the United Nations, but rather where a child of God prays in the power of the Spirit for God's will to be done in her life, in her home, and in the world around her.

Ruth Bell Graham

We must leave it to God to answer our prayers in His own wisest way. Sometimes, we are so impatient and think that God does not answer. God always answers! He never fails! Be still. Abide in Him.

Mrs. Charles E. Cowman

Are you weak? Weary? Confused? Troubled? Pressured? How is your relationship with God? Is it held in its place of priority? I believe the greater the pressure, the greater your need for time alone with Him.

Kay Arthur

When there is a matter that requires definite prayer, pray until you believe God and until you can thank Him for His answer.

Hannah Whitall Smith

When the Holy Spirit comes to dwell within us, I believe we gain a built-in inclination to take our concerns and needs to the Lord in prayer.

Shirley Dobson

## More from God's Word

*The intense prayer of the righteous is very powerful.*

James 5:16 HCSB


*Let the words of my mouth and the meditation of my heart be acceptable in Your sight, O Lord, my strength and my Redeemer.*

Psalm 19:14 NKJV


*Yet He often withdrew to deserted places and prayed.*

Luke 5:16 HCSB


*Rejoice in hope; be patient in affliction; be persistent in prayer.*

Romans 12:12 HCSB


*Ask, and it shall be given you; seek, and ye shall find; knock, and it shall be opened unto you: for every one that asketh receiveth; and he that seeketh findeth; and to him that knocketh it shall be opened.*

Matthew 7:7-8 KJV

## A Prayer

*Dear Lord, Your Holy Word commands me to pray without ceasing. Let me take everything to You in prayer. When I am discouraged, let me pray. When I am lonely, let me take my sorrows to You. When I grieve, let me take my tears to You, Father, in prayer. And when I am joyful, let me offer up prayers of thanksgiving. In all things great and small, at all times, whether happy or sad, let me seek Your wisdom and Your grace . . . in prayer. Amen*

### Easy-and-Good Candied Buckeyes

1 12-ounce package of chocolate chips
3 cups confectioner's sugar (sifted)
1 cup of peanut butter (smooth)
1 stick of butter

Mix sugar, butter, and peanut butter, and form into small balls. Melt chocolate. Dip balls into melted chocolate. Cool in refrigerator until chocolate hardens.

# Chapter 8

# Patience Inside (and Outside) the Kitchen

*Patience is better than power,*
*and controlling one's temper, than capturing a city.*
Proverbs 16:32 HCSB

### Today's Big Idea

When you learn to be more patient
with others, you'll make your world—
and your home—a better place.

We human beings are, by our very nature, impatient. We are impatient with others, impatient with ourselves, and impatient with our Creator. We want things to happen in a certain way and in accordance with our own timetables, but our Heavenly Father may have other plans. That's why we must learn the art of patience.

Are you one of those women who demands perfection from everybody, especially yourself? If so, it's time to lighten up, whether you're in the kitchen, at church, at the workplace, or anyplace in between.

The difference between perfectionism and excellence is the difference between a life of frustration and a life of satisfaction. Only one earthly being ever lived life to perfection, and He was the Son of God. The rest of us have fallen short of God's standard and need to be accepting of our own limitations as well as the limitations of others. God is perfect; we human beings are not. May we live—and forgive—accordingly.

## A Timely Tip

Kids imitate their parents, so act accordingly! The best way for your child to learn to be patient is by example . . . your example!

## *More Ideas about Patience*

Let me encourage you to continue to wait with faith. God may not perform a miracle, but He is trustworthy to touch you and make you whole where there used to be a hole.

Lisa Whelchel

Waiting is the hardest kind of work, but God knows best, and we may joyfully leave all in His hands.

Lottie Moon

Wisdom always waits for the right time to act, while emotion always pushes for action right now.

Joyce Meyer

How do you wait upon the Lord? First you must learn to sit at His feet and take time to listen to His words.

Kay Arthur

We must learn to wait. There is grace supplied to the one who waits.

Mrs. Charles E. Cowman

When I am dealing with an all-powerful, all-knowing God, I, as a mere mortal, must offer my petitions not only with persistence, but also with patience. Someday I'll know why.

Ruth Bell Graham

Patience endurance attains to all things. The one who possesses God is lacking in nothing; God alone is enough.

St. Teresa of Avila

It is wise to wait because God gives clear direction only when we are willing to wait.

Charles Stanley

When we read of the great Biblical leaders, we see that it was not uncommon for God to ask them to wait, not just a day or two, but for years, until God was ready for them to act.

Gloria Gaither

## *More from God's Word*

*Rejoice in hope; be patient in affliction; be persistent in prayer.*

Romans 12:12 HCSB

*Love is patient; love is kind.*

1 Corinthians 13:4 HCSB

*A patient spirit is better than a proud spirit.*

Ecclesiastes 7:8 HCSB

*Therefore the Lord is waiting to show you mercy, and is rising up to show you compassion, for the Lord is a just God. Happy are all who wait patiently for Him.*

Isaiah 30:18 HCSB

*A patient person [shows] great understanding, but a quick-tempered one promotes foolishness.*

Proverbs 14:29 HCSB

## A Prayer

*Dear Lord, give me wisdom and patience. When I am hurried, give me peace. When I am frustrated, give me perspective. When I am angry, keep me mindful of Your presence. Today, let me be a patient Christian, Lord, as I trust in You and in Your master plan for my life. Amen*

## Tasty-and-Tangy Potato Salad

6 large potatoes
1 stalk of celery
3 small onions (chopped)
Salad dressing or mayonnaise
Salt and pepper (to taste)

2 small jars of pimientos
6 eggs (boiled)
Small jar of relish

Boil potatoes with skin on; allow potatoes to cool, then peel and dice. Boil eggs and allow to cool; chop up eggs. Chop celery and onions. Add all ingredients together, mix well, add salad dressing or mayonnaise to taste. For a little extra zest, consider adding two teaspoons of pickle juice. Chill and serve.

# Chapter 9

# Celebrating God's Abundance

*I have come that they may have life,
and that they may have it more abundantly.*

John 10:10 NKJV

### *Today's Big Idea*

God wants to shower you and your family
with abundance—your job is to let Him.

The familiar words of John 10:10 should serve as a daily reminder: Christ came to this earth so that we might experience His abundance, His love, and His gift of eternal life. But Christ does not force Himself upon us; we must claim His gifts for ourselves.

Every woman knows that some days are so busy and so hurried that abundance seems a distant promise. It is not. Every day, we can claim the spiritual abundance that God promises for our lives . . . and we should.

Thomas Brooks spoke for believers of every generation when he observed, "Christ is the sun, and all the watches of our lives should be set by the dial of his motion." Christ, indeed, is the ultimate Savior of mankind and the personal Savior of those who believe in Him. As His servants, we should place Him at the very center of our lives. And, every day that God gives us breath, we should share Christ's love and His abundance with a world that needs both.

## A Timely Tip

Jesus came to give us abundant life, to change the quality of our existence. Our job, of course, is to obey, to pray, to work, and to accept His abundance with open arms.

## *More Ideas about God's Abundance*

God is the giver, and we are the receivers. And His richest gifts are bestowed not upon those who do the greatest things, but upon those who accept His abundance and His grace.

Hannah Whitall Smith

The gift of God is eternal life, spiritual life, abundant life through faith in Jesus Christ, the Living Word of God.

Anne Graham Lotz

It would be wrong to have a "poverty complex," for to think ourselves paupers is to deny either the King's riches or to deny our being His children.

Catherine Marshall

God's riches are beyond anything we could ask or even dare to imagine! If my life gets gooey and stale, I have no excuse.

Barbara Johnson

Get ready for God to show you not only His pleasure, but His approval.

*Joni Eareckson Tada*

People, places, and things were never meant to give us life. God alone is the author of a fulfilling life.

*Gary Smalley & John Trent*

The only way you can experience abundant life is to surrender your plans to Him.

*Charles Stanley*

Instead of living a black-and-white existence, we'll be released into a Technicolor world of vibrancy and emotion when we more accurately reflect His nature to the world around us.

*Bill Hybels*

Jesus wants Life for us, Life with a capital L.

*John Eldredge*

## More from God's Word

*Until now you have asked for nothing in My name. Ask and you will receive, that your joy may be complete.*

John 16:24 HCSB

*And God is able to make every grace overflow to you, so that in every way, always having everything you need, you may excel in every good work.*

2 Corinthians 9:8 HCSB

*My cup runs over. Surely goodness and mercy shall follow me all the days of my life; and I will dwell in the house of the Lord forever.*

Psalm 23:5-6 NKJV

*Ask and it will be given to you; seek and you will find; knock and the door will be opened to you. For everyone who asks receives; he who seeks finds; and to him who knocks, the door will be opened.*

Matthew 7:7-8 NIV

## A Prayer

*Dear Lord, You have offered me the gift of abundance through Your Son. Thank You, Father, for the abundant life that is mine through Christ Jesus. Let me accept His gifts and use them always to glorify You. Amen*

## Old-Fashioned Banana Tea Cake

¼ cup shortening
¼ cup granulated sugar
1 egg, beaten
1 cup milk

¼ teaspoon salt
2 cups flour, sifted
1 ½ to 2 cups mashed bananas
4 teaspoons baking powder

Blend the sugar with shortening and beaten egg. Sift baking powder, salt, and flour together. Combine both mixtures and add milk. Mix the batter well and then fold in the bananas. Pour the batter into a greased and floured 9-inch pan.

Sprinkle with the following topping:
½ cup granulated sugar blended with 2 teaspoons cinnamon.

Preheat oven to 400°; bake for 30 minutes or until done.

# Chapter 10

# Every Day
# Thanksgiving

*Give thanks in all circumstances;*
*for this is God's will for you in Christ Jesus.*
1 Thessalonians 5:18 NIV

### Today's Big Idea

You owe God everything . . .
including your thanks.

I f you've spent much time in the kitchen, you've probably cooked your fair share of holiday feasts, including the granddaddy of them all: Thanksgiving dinner. But as a Christian, you have clear instructions to make every day of the year a cause for thanksgiving, not just the fourth Thursday in November.

Sometimes, life here on earth can be complicated, demanding, and busy. When the demands of life leave us rushing from place to place with scarcely a moment to spare, we may fail to pause and say a word of thanks for all the good things we've received. But when we fail to count our blessings, we rob ourselves of the happiness, the peace, and the gratitude that should rightfully be ours.

So today, even if you're busily engaged in life, slow down long enough to start counting your blessings. You most certainly will not be able to count them all, but take a few moments to jot down as many blessings as you can. Then, give thanks to the Giver of all good things: God. His love for you is eternal, as are His gifts. And it's never too soon—or too late—to offer Him thanks.

## A Timely Tip

By speaking words of thanksgiving and praise, you honor the Father and you protect your heart against the twin evils of apathy and ingratitude.

## *More Ideas about Thanksgiving*

God is worthy of our praise and is pleased when we come before Him with thanksgiving.

Shirley Dobson

The act of thanksgiving is a demonstration of the fact that you are going to trust and believe God.

Kay Arthur

The joy of the Holy Spirit is experienced by giving thanks in all situations.

Bill Bright

The words "thank" and "think" come from the same root word. If we would think more, we would thank more.

Warren Wiersbe

God often keeps us on the path by guiding us through the counsel of friends and trusted spiritual advisors.

Bill Hybels

Thanksgiving or complaining—these words express two contrastive attitudes of the souls of God's children in regard to His dealings with them. The soul that gives thanks can find comfort in everything; the soul that complains can find comfort in nothing.

Hannah Whitall Smith

Thanksgiving is good but Thanksliving is better.

Jim Gallery

If you won't fill your heart with gratitude, the devil will fill it with something else.

Marie T. Freeman

## *More from God's Word*

*Thanks be to God for His indescribable gift.*

2 Corinthians 9:15 HCSB

*And let the peace of the Messiah, to which you were also called in one body, control your hearts. Be thankful.*

Colossians 3:15 HCSB

*Therefore as you have received Christ Jesus the Lord, walk in Him, rooted and built up in Him and established in the faith, just as you were taught, and overflowing with thankfulness.*

Colossians 2:6-7 HCSB

*It is good to give thanks to the Lord, and to sing praises to Your name, O Most High.*

Psalm 92:1 NKJV

*Enter into His gates with thanksgiving, and into His courts with praise. Be thankful to Him, and bless His name. For the Lord is good; His mercy is everlasting, and His truth endures to all generations.*

Psalm 100:4-5 NKJV

## A Prayer

*Dear Lord, sometimes, amid the demands of the day, I lose perspective, and I fail to give thanks for Your blessings and for Your love. Today, help me to count those blessings, and let me give thanks to You, Father, for Your love, for Your grace, for Your blessings, and for Your Son. Amen*

## Cheesy Baked Squash

| | |
|---|---|
| 2 ½ pounds of squash | ½ cup grated cheddar cheese |
| ¼ cup chopped onions | ½ cup cracker crumbs |
| ½ cup sour cream | Salt and pepper (to taste) |

Slice squash and cook in salted water until tender; drain well and mash squash. Stir onion, sour cream, and cheese into squash. Pour mixture into baking dish and cover with crumbs. Bake at 350° for 30 minutes.

# Chapter 11

# Finding Purpose in the Kitchen . . . and Out

*You reveal the path of life to me;*
*in Your presence is abundant joy;*
*in Your right hand are eternal pleasures.*
Psalm 16:11 HCSB

## Today's Big Idea

God has a plan for your life, a definite purpose
that you can fulfill . . . or not. Your challenge is to pray
for God's guidance and to follow wherever He leads.

"What on earth does God intend for me to do with my life?" It's an easy question to ask but, for many of us, a difficult question to answer. Why? Because God's purposes aren't always clear to us. Sometimes we wander aimlessly in a wilderness of our own making. Or sometimes, we may feel trapped in our jobs—or in our kitchens! On other occasions, we may even struggle against God in an unsuccessful attempt to find success and happiness through our own means, not His.

If you're a woman who sincerely seeks God's guidance, He will give it. But, He will make His revelations known to you in a way and in a time of His choosing, not yours, so be patient. If you prayerfully petition God and work diligently to discern His intentions, He will, in time, lead you to a place of joyful abundance and eternal peace.

Sometimes, God's intentions will be clear to you; other times, God's plan will seem uncertain at best. But even on those difficult days when you are unsure which way to turn, you must never lose sight of these overriding facts: God created you for a reason; He has important work for you to do; and He's waiting patiently for you to do it. The next step is up to you.

## A Timely Tip

Discovering God's purpose for your life requires a willingness to be open. God's plan is unfolding day by day. If you keep your eyes and your heart open, He'll reveal His plans. God has big things in store for you, but He may have quite a few lessons to teach you before you are fully prepared to do His will and fulfill His purposes.

## More Ideas about Finding Purpose

Yesterday is just experience but tomorrow is glistening with purpose—and today is the channel leading from one to the other.

Barbara Johnson

Only God's chosen task for you will ultimately satisfy. Do not wait until it is too late to realize the privilege of serving Him in His chosen position for you.

Beth Moore

His life is our light—our purpose and meaning and reason for living.

Anne Graham Lotz

In the very place where God has put us, whatever its limitations, whatever kind of work it may be, we may indeed serve the Lord Christ.

Elisabeth Elliot

God custom-designed you with your unique combination of personality, temperament, talents, and background, and He wants to harness and use these in His mission to reach this messed-up world.

Bill Hybels

We aren't just thrown on this earth like dice tossed across a table. We are lovingly placed here for a purpose.

Charles Swindoll

Blessed are those who know what on earth they are here on earth to do and set themselves about the business of doing it.

Max Lucado

Aim at Heaven and you will get earth "thrown in"; aim at earth and you will get neither.

C. S. Lewis

## *More from God's Word*

*For it is God who is working among you both the willing and the working for His good purpose.*

Philippians 2:13 HCSB

*We know that all things work together for the good of those who love God: those who are called according to His purpose.*

Romans 8:28 HCSB

*I will instruct you and show you the way to go; with My eye on you, I will give counsel.*

Psalm 32:8 HCSB

*To everything there is a season, a time for every purpose under heaven.*

Ecclesiastes 3:1 NKJV

*Commit your activities to the Lord and your plans will be achieved.*

Proverbs 16:3 HCSB

## A Prayer

*Dear Lord, let Your purposes be my purposes. Let Your priorities be my priorities. Let Your will be my will. Let Your Word be my guide. And, let me grow in faith and in wisdom today and every day. Amen*

## Picnic-Style Deviled Eggs

4 hard-boiled eggs
¼ teaspoon cayenne pepper
¼ teaspoon salt
1 teaspoon white vinegar
1 teaspoon olive oil or melted butter
½ teaspoon mustard

Boil eggs, then chill. When eggs are cold, remove shell and cut each egg in half (lengthwise). Remove yolks and set whites aside. Rub yokes smooth and then mix yolks with remaining ingredients. Roll yolk mixture into balls and place in whites. For a little flair, serve over a bed of crisp lettuce.

# Chapter 12

# When Things Don't Work Out

*God is our refuge and strength,*
*a very present help in trouble.*
Psalm 46:1 NKJV

*Today's Big Idea*

When times are tough,
you should guard your heart
by turning it over to God.

All of us face times of adversity. Sometimes our challenges are minor: the cake falls flatter than a pancake, and we end up with egg on our faces, but nobody is really hurt. On other occasions, things turn far more serious, and we must endure the disappointments and tragedies that befall believers and nonbelievers alike.

When we face the inevitable difficulties of life here on earth, God stands ready to protect us. Our responsibility, of course, is to ask Him for protection. When we call upon Him in heartfelt prayer, He will answer—in His own time and according to His own plan—and He will heal us. And while we are waiting for God's plans to unfold and for His healing touch to restore us, we can be comforted in the knowledge that our Creator can overcome any obstacle, even if we cannot. Let us take God at His word, and let us trust Him today, tomorrow, and forever.

## A Timely Tip

All families endure times of sadness or hardship; if your troubles seem overwhelming, be willing to seek outside help—starting, of course, with your pastor.

## *More Ideas about Tough Times*

Life is simply hard. That's all there is to it. Thank goodness, the intensity of difficulty rises and falls. Some seasons are far more bearable than others, but none is without challenge.

Beth Moore

We all go through pain and sorrow, but the presence of God, like a warm, comforting blanket, can shield us and protect us, and allow the deep inner joy to surface, even in the most devastating circumstances.

Barbara Johnson

Often the trials we mourn are really gateways into the good things we long for.

Hannah Whitall Smith

If we make our troubles an opportunity to learn more of God's love and His power to aid and bless, then they will teach us to have a firmer confidence in His Providence.

Billy Graham

Recently I've been learning that life comes down to this: God is in everything. Regardless of what difficulties I am experiencing at the moment, or what things aren't as I would like them to be, I look at the circumstances and say, "Lord, what are you trying to teach me?"

Catherine Marshall

If God sends us on stony paths, he provides strong shoes.

Corrie ten Boom

This hard place in which you perhaps find yourself is the very place in which God is giving you opportunity to look only to Him, to spend time in prayer, and to learn long-suffering, gentleness, meekness—in short, to learn the depths of the love that Christ Himself has poured out on all of us.

Elisabeth Elliot

Often God shuts a door in our face so that he can open the door through which he wants us to go.

Catherine Marshall

## *More from God's Word*

*When you are in distress and all these things have happened to you, you will return to the Lord your God in later days and obey Him. He will not leave you, destroy you, or forget the covenant with your fathers that He swore to them by oath, because the Lord your God is a compassionate God.*

Deuteronomy 4:30-31 HCSB

*Whatever has been born of God conquers the world. This is the victory that has conquered the world: our faith.*

1 John 5:4 HCSB

*Dear friends, when the fiery ordeal arises among you to test you, don't be surprised by it, as if something unusual were happening to you. Instead, as you share in the sufferings of the Messiah rejoice, so that you may also rejoice with great joy at the revelation of His glory.*

1 Peter 4:12-13 HCSB

*We are pressured in every way but not crushed; we are perplexed but not in despair.*

2 Corinthians 4:8 HCSB

## A Prayer

*Dear Heavenly Father, You are my strength and my protector. When I am troubled, You comfort me. When I am discouraged, You lift me up. When I am afraid, You deliver me. Let me turn to You, Lord, when I am weak. In times of adversity, let me trust Your plan and Your will for my life. Your love is infinite, as is Your wisdom. Whatever my circumstances, Dear Lord, let me always give the praise, and the thanks, and the glory to You. Amen*

### Old-Time Florida Orange Marmalade Breakfast Spread

8 oranges                     8 cups sugar
2 lemons

Cut up oranges and lemons (fine) and soak in 12 cups of water for 24 hours. Then, boil mixture for 2 hours. Add sugar and boil for another 1½ hours or until thick. Tastes great on toast or English muffins!

# Chapter 13

# Home Is Where the Heart Is

*Unless the Lord builds a house, its builders labor over it in vain; unless the Lord watches over a city, the watchman stays alert in vain.*

Psalm 127:1 HCSB

## Today's Big Idea

God wants your home to be a joyous place filled with praise and celebration.

As every woman knows, family life is a mixture of conversations, mediations, irritations, deliberations, commiserations, frustrations, negotiations and celebrations. In other words, providing a loving home for our loved ones is an incredibly varied job.

Certainly, in the life of every family, there are moments of frustration and disappointment. Lots of them. But, for those who are lucky enough to live in the presence of a close-knit, caring clan, the rewards far outweigh the frustrations.

No family is perfect, and neither is yours. But, despite the inevitable challenges and occasional hurt feelings of family life, your clan is God's gift to you. That little band of men, women, kids, and babies is a priceless treasure on temporary loan from the Father above. Give thanks to the Giver for the gift of family . . . and act accordingly.

## A Timely Tip

Make this day and every day a celebration. Put God first and make your home a sanctuary, a place filled with love and laughter.

## More Ideas about Your Home and Your Loved Ones

The secret of a happy home life is that the members of the family learn to give and receive love.

Billy Graham

Home is not only where the heart is; it is also where the happiness is.

Marie T. Freeman

God's peace is like a river, not a pond. In other words, a sense of health and well-being, both of which are expressions of the Hebrew *shalom*, can permeate our homes even when we're in white-water rapids.

Beth Moore

When God asks someone to do something for Him entailing sacrifice, he makes up for it in surprising ways. Though He has led Bill all over the world to preach the gospel, He has not forgotten the little family in the mountains of North Carolina.

Ruth Bell Graham

Whatever else maybe said about the home, it is the bottom line of life, the anvil upon which attitudes and convictions are hammered out.

Charles Swindoll

The home should be a kind of church, a place where God is honored.

Billy Graham

God, give us Christian homes! Homes where the Bible is loved and taught, homes where the Master's will is sought.

B. B. McKinney

To go home is to be refreshed in my spirit and refocused in my thoughts and renewed in my strength and restored in my heart.

Anne Graham Lotz

What can we do to promote world peace? Go home and love your family.

Mother Teresa

## *More from God's Word*

*It takes knowledge to fill a home with rare and beautiful treasures.*

Proverbs 24:4 NCV

*Hear, O Israel: The LORD our God, the LORD is one. Love the LORD your God with all your heart and with all your soul and with all your strength. These commandments that I give you today are to be upon your hearts. Impress them on your children. Talk about them when you sit at home and when you walk along the road, when you lie down and when you get up.*

Deuteronomy 6:4-7 NIV

*Choose for yourselves today the one you will worship . . . . As for me and my family, we will worship the Lord.*

Joshua 24:15 HCSB

*The one who blesses others is abundantly blessed; those who help others are helped.*

Proverbs 11:25 MSG

## *A Prayer*

*Dear Lord, I thank You for my home and for my family. I have been blessed with a loving family and faithful friends. Today and every day, let me show them that I love them by the things that I say and the things that I do. Amen*

# Holiday Eggnog

8 eggs

3 cups milk

2 cups whipping cream

1¼ cup sugar

½ teaspoon vanilla extract

¼ teaspoon ground nutmeg

Using an electric mixer, beat the eggs for 2 or 3 minutes (until frothy). While mixing, gradually add sugar, vanilla and nutmeg. Turn the mixer off and stir in whipping cream and milk. Chill eggnog and sprinkle individual servings with additional nutmeg.

# Chapter 14

# Finding Moments of Peace

*Peace I leave with you, My peace I give to you;*
*not as the world gives do I give to you.*
*Let not your heart be troubled, neither let it be afraid.*

John 14:27 NKJV

*Today's Big Idea*

God's peace surpasses human understanding.
When you accept His peace,
it will revolutionize your life.

If you're a savvy chef, you know what it takes to manage your kitchen. But when it comes to managing life outside the kitchen, things aren't quite so simple. You live in a complicated society filled with distractions and temptations. No wonder it can be difficult to find peace and even harder to keep it.

Have you discovered the genuine peace that can be yours through Jesus Christ? Or are you still rushing after the illusion of "peace and happiness" that the world promises but cannot deliver?

Today, as a gift to yourself, to your family, and to the world, let Christ's peace become your peace. Let Him rule your heart, your thoughts, and your life. When you do, you will partake in the peace that only He can give.

So the next time you journey out into the chaos of the world, bring God's peace with you. And remember: the chaos is temporary, but God's peace is not.

## A Timely Tip

Sometimes peace is a scarce commodity in a demanding, 21st-century world. How can we find the peace that we so desperately desire? By turning our days and our lives over to God. Whatever it is, God can handle it.

## *More Ideas about Finding Peace*

Prayer guards hearts and minds and causes God to bring peace out of chaos.

Beth Moore

The fruit of our placing all things in God's hands is the presence of His abiding peace in our hearts.

Hannah Whitall Smith

In the center of a hurricane there is absolute quiet and peace. There is no safer place than in the center of the will of God.

Corrie ten Boom

Thou hast formed us for Thyself, and our hearts are restless till they find rest in Thee.

St. Augustine

Peace is the deepest thing a human personality can know; it is almighty.

Oswald Chambers

I believe that in every time and place it is within our power to acquiesce in the will of God—and what peace it brings to do so!

Elisabeth Elliot

To know God as He really is—in His essential nature and character—is to arrive at a citadel of peace that circumstances may storm, but can never capture.

Catherine Marshall

We're prone to want God to change our circumstances, but He wants to change our character. We think that peace comes from the outside in, but it comes from the inside out.

Warren Wiersbe

What peace can they have who are not at peace with God?

Matthew Henry

## More from God's Word

*The result of righteousness will be peace; the effect of righteousness will be quiet confidence forever.*

Isaiah 32:17 HCSB

*Grace, mercy, and peace will be with us from God the Father and from Jesus Christ, the Son of the Father, in truth and love.*

2 John 1:3 HCSB

*And let the peace of the Messiah, to which you were also called in one body, control your hearts. Be thankful.*

Colossians 3:15 HCSB

*But now in Christ Jesus, you who were far away have been brought near by the blood of the Messiah. For He is our peace, who made both groups one and tore down the dividing wall of hostility.*

Ephesians 2:13-14 HCSB

## A Prayer

*Dear Lord, I will open my heart to You. And I thank You, God, for Your love, for Your peace, and for Your Son. Amen*

### Crowd-Pleasing Banana Pudding

| | |
|---|---|
| 4 ripe bananas (sliced) | Dash of salt |
| 2 cups whole milk | 1 teaspoon vanilla |
| 3 eggs (beaten) | 2 tablespoons cornstarch |
| 1 cup sugar | Vanilla wafers |

Mix eggs and sugar well and then add cornstarch, milk, and salt. Bring this mixture to a boil over medium to medium-high heat; as the mixture begins to boil, stir constantly; continue cooking until the mixture thickens. Remove mixture from heat and stir in vanilla (make sure vanilla is mixed in thoroughly). Layer the vanilla wafers, the pudding, and the sliced bananas in serving bowl. Enjoy!

# Chapter 15

# Working in the Kitchen, Working in the World

*Be strong and courageous, and do the work.*
*Don't be afraid or discouraged, for the Lord God, my God,*
*is with you. He won't leave you or forsake you.*

1 Chronicles 28:20 HCSB

## Today's Big Idea

When you find work that pleases God—
and when you apply yourself conscientiously
to the job at hand—you'll be rewarded.

Cooking for your family and providing for your loved ones requires work. Lots of work. And whether or not your work carries you outside the home, your good deeds have earned the gratitude of your loved ones and the praise of your Heavenly Father.

It has been said that there are no shortcuts to any place worth going. Mothers agree. Making the grade in today's competitive workplace is not easy. In fact, it can be very difficult indeed. The same can be said for the important work that occurs within the four walls of your home.

God did not create you and your family for lives of mediocrity; He created you for far greater things. Accomplishing God's work is seldom easy. What's required is determination, persistence, patience, and discipline—which is perfectly fine with God. After all, He knows that you're up to the task, and He has big plans for all of you. Very big plans . . .

## A Timely Tip

It has been said that there are no shortcuts to any place worth going. Hard work is not simply a proven way to get ahead, it's also part of God's plan for all His children (including you).

## More Ideas about Work

Ordinary work, which is what most of us do most of the time, is ordained by God every bit as much as is the extraordinary.

Elisabeth Elliot

You can't climb the ladder of life with your hands in your pockets.

Barbara Johnson

Great relief and satisfaction can come from seeking God's priorities for us in each season, discerning what is "best" in the midst of many noble opportunities, and pouring our most excellent energies into those things.

Beth Moore

In the very place where God has put us, whatever its limitations, whatever kind of work it may be, we may indeed serve the Lord Christ.

Elisabeth Elliot

If you honor God with your work, He will honor you because of your work.

Marie T. Freeman

Few things fire up a person's commitment like dedication to excellence.

John Maxwell

Thank God every morning when you get up that you have something which must be done, whether you like it or not. Work breeds a hundred virtues that idleness never knows.

Charles Kingsley

It may be that the day of judgment will dawn tomorrow; in that case, we shall gladly stop working for a better tomorrow. But not before.

Dietrich Bonhoeffer

God provides the ingredients for our daily bread but expects us to do the baking. With our own hands!

Barbara Johnson

## *More from God's Word*

*Whatever you do, do it enthusiastically, as something done for the Lord and not for men.*

Colossians 3:23 HCSB

*Whatever your hands find to do, do with [all] your strength.*

Ecclesiastes 9:10 HCSB

*He did it with all his heart. So he prospered.*

2 Chronicles 31:21 NKJV

*Don't work only while being watched, in order to please men, but as slaves of Christ, do God's will from your heart. Render service with a good attitude, as to the Lord and not to men.*

Ephesians 6:6-7 HCSB

*We must do the works of Him who sent Me while it is day. Night is coming when no one can work.*

John 9:4 HCSB

## A Prayer

*Dear Lord, make my work pleasing to You. Help me to sow the seeds of Your abundance everywhere I go. Let me be diligent in all my undertakings and give me patience to wait for Your harvest. Amen*

## Cheesy Rice

1 cup uncooked rice                ½ cup finely chopped onion
½ stick of butter                                 3 tablespoons flour
1 teaspoon salt                       8 to 12 ounces grated cheese
2 cups whole milk                      Dash of pepper (optional)
½ teaspoon Worcestershire sauce (optional)
Soft bread crumbs for topping

Cook rice using package directions. While rice is cooking, sauté onion in butter; blend in flour, salt, pepper (optional), and Worcestershire sauce (optional). Next, slowly add milk, stirring constantly. Then, add this entire mixture to the rice and mix all ingredients together thoroughly. Pour into baking dish and cover with crumbs. Bake at 350° for 30 minutes.

# Chapter 16

# Another Day in the Kitchen . . . Another Cause for Celebration

*This is the day the Lord has made;*
*let us rejoice and be glad in it.*
Psalm 118:24 HCSB

## Today's Big Idea

Today is a wonderful, one-of-a-kind gift
from God. Treat it that way.

Life in the kitchen—or outside it—should never be taken for granted. Each day is a priceless gift from God and should be treated as such.

Do you approach each day with celebration or with reservation? If you are a believer who has been redeemed by a loving Savior, the answer should be obvious. Each day should be a cause for celebration and for praise.

Thoughtful Christians should be joyful Christians. And even on life's darker days, even during those difficult times when we scarcely see a single ray of sunlight, we can still praise God and thank Him for our blessings. When we do, we demonstrate that our acquaintance with the Master is not a passing fancy, but is, instead, the cornerstone and the touchstone of our lives.

## A Timely Tip

Take time to celebrate another day of life. And while you're at it, encourage your family and friends to join in the celebration.

## *More Ideas about Celebrating Today*

When your life comes to a close, you will remember not days but moments. Treasure each one.

Barbara Johnson

Commitment to His lordship on Easter, at revivals, or even every Sunday is not enough. We must choose this day—and every day—whom we will serve. This deliberate act of the will is the inevitable choice between habitual fellowship and habitual failure.

Beth Moore

With each new dawn, life delivers a package to your front door, rings your doorbell, and runs.

Charles Swindoll

Today is mine. Tomorrow is none of my business. If I peer anxiously into the fog of the future, I will strain my spiritual eyes so that I will not see clearly what is required of me now.

Elisabeth Elliot

How much of our lives are, well, so daily. How often our hours are filled with the mundane, seemingly unimportant things that have to be done, whether at home or work. These very "daily" tasks could become a celebration of praise. "It is through consecration," someone has said, "that drudgery is made divine."

Gigi Graham Tchividjian

Each day, each moment is so pregnant with eternity that if we "tune in" to it, we can hardly contain the joy.

Gloria Gaither

Submit each day to God, knowing that He is God over all your tomorrows.

Kay Arthur

Every day we live is a priceless gift of God, loaded with possibilities to learn something new, to gain fresh insights.

Dale Evans Rogers

Every day of our lives we make choices about how we're going to live that day.

Luci Swindoll

## More from God's Word

*Working together with Him, we also appeal to you: "Don't receive God's grace in vain." For He says: In an acceptable time, I heard you, and in the day of salvation, I helped you. Look, now is the acceptable time; look, now is the day of salvation.*

2 Corinthians 6:1-2 HCSB

*I must work the works of Him who sent Me while it is day; the night is coming when no one can work.*

John 9:4 NKJV

*Therefore, get your minds ready for action, being self-disciplined, and set your hope completely on the grace to be brought to you at the revelation of Jesus Christ.*

1 Peter 1:13 HCSB

*So teach us to number our days, that we may gain a heart of wisdom.*

Psalm 90:12 NKJV

## A Prayer

*Dear Lord, You have given me another day of life; let me celebrate this day, and let me use it according to Your plan. I come to You today with faith in my heart and praise on my lips. I praise You, Father, for the gift of life and for the friends and family members who make my life rich. Enable me to live each moment to the fullest, totally involved in Your will. Amen*

## Crowd-Pleasing Fruit Tea

| | |
|---|---|
| 5 tea bags | 3 quarts water |
| 1 cup sugar | 1 large can pineapple juice |
| 1 quart orange juice | 2 lemons |

Put 1 quart of the water in a saucepan; bring to a boil and add tea bags. Remove the tea bags. Put sugar in a large tea pitcher; pour the hot brewed tea over the sugar and stir until totally dissolved. Then, pour sweetened mixture into a punch bowl. Add orange juice, pineapple juice, and remaining water. Cut lemons and squeeze juice into the mixture. Stir and serve. Makes about 20 8-ounce servings.

# Chapter 17

# Trusting God's Recipes

*Your word is a lamp for my feet
and a light on my path.*
Psalm 119:105 HCSB

## Today's Big Idea

God's wisdom is perfect, and it's available to you.
So if you want to become wise, become a student of
God's Word and a follower of His Son.

What book contains infallible recipes for life here on earth and life eternal? The Bible, of course. And as Christians, we are called upon to share God's Holy Word with a world in desperate need of His healing hand.

Vance Havner observed, "It takes calm, thoughtful, prayerful meditation on the Word to extract its deepest nourishment." How true. God's Word can be a roadmap to a place of righteousness and abundance. Make it your roadmap. God's wisdom can be a light to guide your steps. Claim it as your light today, tomorrow, and every day of your life—and then walk confidently in the footsteps of God's only begotten Son.

## A Timely Tip

Trust God's Word: Charles Swindoll writes, "There are four words I wish we would never forget, and they are, 'God keeps his word.'" And remember: When it comes to studying God's Word, school is always in session.

## *More Ideas about God's Word*

I need the spiritual revival that comes from spending quiet time alone with Jesus in prayer and in thoughtful meditation on His Word.

Anne Graham Lotz

Only through routine, regular exposure to God's Word can you and I draw out the nutrition needed to grow a heart of faith.

Elizabeth George

One of the greatest ways God changes me is by bringing Scripture to mind that I have hidden deep in my heart. And, He always picks the right Scripture at the right time.

Evelyn Christianson

Weave the unveiling fabric of God's word through your heart and mind. It will hold strong, even if the rest of life unravels.

Gigi Graham Tchividjian

God's Word is not merely letters on paper . . . it's alive. Believe and draw near, for it longs to dance in your heart and whisper to you in the night.

Lisa Bevere

God can see clearly no matter how dark or foggy the night is. Trust His Word to guide you safely home.

Lisa Whelchel

Words fail to express my love for this holy Book, my gratitude for its author, for His love and goodness. How shall I thank him for it?

Lottie Moon

The Bible became a living book and a guide for my life.

Vonette Bright

God meant that we adjust to the Gospel—not the other way around.

Vance Havner

## More from God's Word

*But the word of the Lord endures forever. And this is the word that was preached as the gospel to you.*

1 Peter 1:25 HCSB

*All Scripture is inspired by God and is profitable for teaching, for rebuking, for correcting, for training in righteousness, so that the man of God may be complete, equipped for every good work.*

2 Timothy 3:16-17 HCSB

*For the word of God is living and effective and sharper than any two-edged sword, penetrating as far as to divide soul, spirit, joints, and marrow; it is a judge of the ideas and thoughts of the heart.*

Hebrews 4:12 HCSB

*The one who is from God listens to God's words. This is why you don't listen, because you are not from God.*

John 8:47 HCSB

## A Prayer

*Heavenly Father, Your Holy Word is a light unto the world; let me study it, trust it, and share it with all who cross my path. In all that I do, help me be a worthy witness for You as I share the Good News of Your perfect Son and Your perfect Word. Amen*

## Homemade Melt-in-Your-Mouth Biscuits

2 cups flour

1 teaspoon salt

1 tablespoon baking powder

¼ cup shortening

¾ cup milk

Sift all dry ingredients together in a large bowl. Cut in shortening. Add milk slowly while stirring (add only enough milk to form a soft dough). Turn the dough onto a floured surface. Knead gently until the mixture forms a smooth ball of dough that is not sticky. Using a floured rolling pin, roll dough to a thickness of ½ inch. Dip biscuit cutter into flour, then cut dough. Place biscuits on ungreased baking sheet (1" apart). Bake at 450° for about 8 to 10 minutes, or until the tops of the biscuits are golden brown.

# Chapter 18

# Finding the Right Recipe . . . for Life

*But seek first the kingdom of God and His righteousness,*
*and all these things will be provided for you.*
Matthew 6:33 HCSB

## Today's Big Idea

Your heavenly Father wants you to prioritize
your day and your life. And the best place to start
is by putting God first.

I f you've formed the habit of making a daily to-do list, then you are, in truth, creating a new (and important) recipe for the coming day. So where does God fit into your plans? Do you "squeeze Him in" on Sundays and at mealtimes? Or do you consult Him on a moment-to-moment basis? The answer to this question will determine the direction of your life's journey, the quality of that journey, and its ultimate destination.

As you make plans for the next 24 hours, organize your life around this simple principle: "God first." When you place your Creator where He belongs—at the very center of your day and your life—the rest of your priorities will, more often than not, fall into place.

## A Timely Tip

Setting priorities may mean saying no. You don't have time to do everything, so it's perfectly okay to say no to the things that mean less so that you'll have time for the things that mean more. So today, spend a few moments asking God to help you prioritize the things you should do . . . and while you're at it, ask Him to help you say no to the things you shouldn't do.

## *More Ideas about Your Priorities*

It's sobering to contemplate how much time, effort, sacrifice, compromise, and attention we give to acquiring and increasing our supply of something that is totally insignificant in eternity.

Anne Graham Lotz

Great relief and satisfaction can come from seeking God's priorities for us in each season, discerning what is "best" in the midst of many noble opportunities, and pouring our most excellent energies into those things.

Beth Moore

Sin is largely a matter of mistaken priorities. Any sin in us that is cherished, hidden, and not confessed will cut the nerve center of our faith.

Catherine Marshall

There were endless demands on Jesus' time. Still he was able to make that amazing claim of "completing the work you gave me to do." (John 17:4 NIV)

Elisabeth Elliot

If choosing to spend time alone with God is a real struggle—a heavy-handed demand that only adds more guilt and stress to your already overblown schedule—it's time to change the way you approach his presence.

Doris Greig

Have you prayed about your resources lately? Find out how God wants you to use your time and your money. No matter what it costs, forsake all that is not of God.

Kay Arthur

Forgetting your mission leads, inevitably, to getting tangled up in details—details that can take you completely off your path.

Laurie Beth Jones

The essence of the Christian life is Jesus: that in all things He might have the preeminence, not that in some things He might have a place.

Franklin Graham

## *More from God's Word*

*Don't abandon wisdom, and she will watch over you; love her, and she will guard you.*

Proverbs 4:6 HCSB

*And I pray this: that your love will keep on growing in knowledge and every kind of discernment, so that you can determine what really matters and can be pure and blameless in the day of Christ.*

Philippians 1:9 HCSB

*So teach us to number our days, that we may gain a heart of wisdom.*

Psalm 90:12 NKJV

*He said to them all, "If anyone desires to come after Me, let him deny himself, and take up his cross daily, and follow Me. For whoever desires to save his life will lose it, but whoever loses his life for My sake will save it."*

Luke 9:23-24 NKJV

## A Prayer

*Dear Lord, make me a person of unwavering commitment to You and to my family. Guide me away from the temptations and distractions of this world, so that I might honor You with my thoughts, my actions, and my prayers. Amen*

## Down Home Pecan Pie

1 cup pecans
¼ cup flour
½ cup whole milk
3 eggs

1 pound light brown sugar
½ teaspoon salt
½ teaspoon vanilla
¾ cup butter (melted)
1 pie crust

Place pecans at the bottom of pie crust. Mix sugar, flour, and salt, and then stir in milk and vanilla. Then, gradually mix in butter and whisk in the eggs, one at a time. Pour mixture over the pecans, then bake at 350° for 1 hr and 15 minutes or until the pie looks done (it should appear puffy and slightly firm around the edges, but not too hard).

# Chapter 19

# And the Greatest of These Is Love

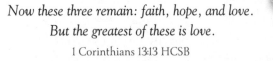

*Now these three remain: faith, hope, and love.*
*But the greatest of these is love.*
1 Corinthians 13:13 HCSB

## Today's Big Idea

God is love, and He expects you to share
His love with others.

The familiar words of 1st Corinthians 13 remind us of the importance of love. Faith is important, of course. So too is hope. But love is more important still.

Christ showed His love for us on the cross, and, as Christians, we are called upon to return Christ's love by sharing it. We are commanded (not advised, not encouraged…commanded!) to love one another just as Christ loved us (John 13:34). That's a tall order, but as Christians, we are obligated to follow it.

Sometimes love is easy (puppies and sleeping children come to mind) and sometimes love is hard (fallible human beings come to mind). But God's Word is clear: We are to love all our friends and neighbors, not just the lovable ones. So today, take time to spread Christ's message by word and by example. And the greatest of these is, of course, is example.

## A Timely Tip

Be expressive. Make certain that at your house, love is expressed and demonstrated many times each day. Little acts of consideration and kindness can make a big difference in the way that your child feels and the way your child behaves.

## *More Ideas about Love*

If Jesus is the preeminent One in our lives, then we will love each other, submit to each other, and treat one another fairly in the Lord.

Warren Wiersbe

Those who abandon ship the first time it enters a storm miss the calm beyond. And the rougher the storms weathered together, the deeper and stronger real love grows.

Ruth Bell Graham

Love is an attribute of God. To love others is evidence of a genuine faith.

Kay Arthur

It is when we come to the Lord in our nothingness, our powerlessness and our helplessness that He then enables us to love in a way which, without Him, would be absolutely impossible.

Elisabeth Elliot

Only joyous love redeems.

Catherine Marshall

Love must be supported and fed and protected, just like a little infant who is growing up at home.

James Dobson

Love is the seed of all hope. It is the enticement to trust, to risk, to try, and to go on.

Gloria Gaither

Love simply cannot spring up without that self-surrender to each other. If either withholds the self, love cannot exist.

E. Stanley Jones

Live your lives in love, the same sort of love which Christ gives us, and which He perfectly expressed when He gave Himself as a sacrifice to God.

Corrie ten Boom

## More from God's Word

*I pray that you, being rooted and firmly established in love, may be able to comprehend with all the saints what is the breadth and width, height and depth, and to know the Messiah's love that surpasses knowledge, so you may be filled with all the fullness of God.*

Ephesians 3:17-19 HCSB

*Beloved, if God so loved us, we also ought to love one another.*

1 John 4:11 NASB

*Love one another deeply, from the heart.*

1 Peter 1:22 NIV

*Above all, love each other deeply, because love covers over a multitude of sins.*

1 Peter 4:8 NIV

*May the Lord cause you to increase and abound in love for one another, and for all people.*

1 Thessalonians 3:12 NASB

## A Prayer

*Lord, You have given me the gift of eternal love; let me share that gift with the world. Help me, Father, to show kindness to those who cross my path, and let me show tenderness and unfailing love to my family and friends. Make me generous with words of encouragement and praise. And, help me always to reflect the love that Christ Jesus gave me so that through me, others might find Him. Amen*

## Hot Fruit Punch

| | |
|---|---|
| 1 quart hot tea | 2 cups sugar |
| 2 cups orange juice | 2 cups pineapple juice |
| 1 cup lemon juice | 2 quarts boiling water |

Dissolve sugar in hot tea. Add juices to tea mixture. Then, add boiling water. Stir and serve hot.

# Chapter 20

# Finding Joy Inside (and Outside) the Kitchen

*These things I have spoken to you, that My joy may remain in you, and that your joy may be full.*

John 15:11 NKJV

## Today's Big Idea

Joy does not depend upon your circumstances; it depends upon your thoughts and upon your relationship with God.

Christ made it clear: He intends that His joy should become our joy. Yet sometimes, amid the inevitable hustle and bustle of life here on earth, we can forfeit—albeit temporarily—the joy of Christ as we wrestle with the challenges of daily living.

Jonathan Edwards, the 18th-century American clergyman, observed, "Christ is not only a remedy for your weariness and trouble, but he will give you an abundance of the contrary: joy and delight. They who come to Christ do not only come to a resting-place after they have been wandering in a wilderness, but they come to a banqueting-house where they may rest, and where they may feast. They may cease from their former troubles and toils, and they may enter upon a course of delights and spiritual joys."

If, today, your heart is heavy, open the door of your soul to Christ. He will give you peace and joy. And, if you already have the joy of Christ in your heart, share it freely, just as Christ freely shared His joy with you.

## A Timely Tip

Joy begins with a choice—the choice to establish a genuine relationship with God and His Son. Joy does not depend upon the ups and downs of everyday life; it depends upon your relationship with the Lord.

## *More Ideas about Experiencing God's Joy*

The Christian lifestyle is not one of legalistic do's and don'ts, but one that is positive, attractive, and joyful.

Vonette Bright

It is the definition of joy to be able to offer back to God the essence of what he's placed in you, be that creativity or a love of ideas or a compassionate heart or the gift of hospitality.

Paula Rinehart

A joyful heart is the inevitable result of a heart burning with love.

Mother Teresa

If you're a thinking Christian, you will be a joyful Christian.

Marie T. Freeman

Finding joy means first of all finding Jesus.

Jill Briscoe

What is your focus today? Joy comes when it is Jesus first, others second…then you.

Kay Arthur

The greatest honor you can give Almighty God is to live gladly and joyfully because of the knowledge of His love.

Juliana of Norwich

I approach prayer in a similar way as I experience the joy of relationship with God. No matter how severe "the winter of the soul" may have been, standing in the presence of God brings pure joy.

Henry Blackaby

Joy is the heart vibrating in grateful rhythm to the love of Almighty God who actually chooses to make His home within us.

Susan Lenzkes

## More from God's Word

*Rejoice in the Lord always. I will say it again: Rejoice!*

Philippians 4:4 HCSB

*Delight yourself also in the Lord, and He shall give you the desires of your heart.*

Psalm 37:4 NKJV

*Make me hear joy and gladness.*

Psalm 51:8 NKJV

*Weeping may spend the night, but there is joy in the morning.*

Psalm 30:5 HCSB

*The Lord reigns; let the earth rejoice.*

Psalm 97:1 NKJV

## A Prayer

*Dear Lord, help me to feel Your joy—and help me to share it—today, tomorrow, and every day. Amen*

## Super-Tasty Rice Pudding

1 cup instant rice, uncooked
2 eggs, beaten
¼ teaspoon nutmeg
¼ teaspoon cinnamon

¼ teaspoon salt
1 cup sugar
2 ½ cups of whole milk
¼ to ½ cup raisins
½ teaspoon vanilla

In a saucepan, combine rice, milk, salt, cinnamon, sugar, and raisins. Bring to a rolling boil, stirring constantly. Reduce heat to a slow boil and cook for 15 minutes while continuing to stir constantly. Then, using a separate container, slowly (and carefully!) pour hot mixture over beaten eggs and stir. Add vanilla to mixture and stir. Place the pudding in a container (or containers) of your choice, sprinkle with nutmeg and allow to cool.

# Chapter 21

# The Power of Hope

*Heaven and earth will pass away,
but My words will never pass away.*
Matthew 24:35 HCSB

## *Today's Big Idea*

Since God has promised to guide and protect you—
now and forever—you should never lose hope.

Are you a hope-filled mom? You should be. After all, God is good; His love endures; and He has blessed you with a loving family. But sometimes, in life's darker moments, you may lose sight of those blessings, and when you do, it's easy to lose hope.

If hope ever becomes a scarce commodity around your house, or if you find yourself falling into the spiritual traps of worry and discouragement, turn your concerns over to God in prayer. Then, seek wisdom and encouragement from trusted friends and family members. And remember this: the world can be a place of trials and tribulations, but God's love conquers all; He has promised you peace, joy, and eternal life. And, of course, God keeps His promises today, tomorrow, and forever, amen!

## A Timely Tip

If you're experiencing hard times, you'll be wise to start spending more time with God. And if you do your part, God will do His part. So never be afraid to hope—or to ask—for a miracle.

## *More Ideas about Hope*

Hope is the desire and the ability to move forward.

Emilie Barnes

Love is the seed of all hope. It is the enticement to trust, to risk, to try, and to go on.

Gloria Gaither

I discovered that sorrow was not to be feared but rather endured with hope and expectancy that God would use it to visit and bless my life.

Jill Briscoe

No other religion, no other philosophy promises new bodies, hearts, and minds. Only in the Gospel of Christ do hurting people find such incredible hope.

Joni Eareckson Tada

Joy lifts our spirit above earth's sorrow, dancing in jubilation at the hope set before us.

Susan Lenzkes

In those desperate times when we feel like we don't have an ounce of strength, He will gently pick up our heads so that our eyes can behold something—something that will keep His hope alive in us.

Kathy Troccoli

The choice for me is to either look at all things I have lost or the things I have. To live in fear or to live in hope.... Hope comes from knowing I have a sovereign, loving God who is in every event in my life.

Lisa Beamer (Her husband Todd was killed on flight 93, 9-11-01)

Never yield to gloomy anticipation. Place your hope and confidence in God. He has no record of failure.

Mrs. Charles E. Cowman

The meaning of hope isn't just some flimsy wishing. It's a firm confidence in God's promises—that he will ultimately set things right.

Sheila Walsh

## More from God's Word

*Let us hold on to the confession of our hope without wavering, for He who promised is faithful.*

Hebrews 10:23 HCSB

*Hope deferred makes the heart sick.*

Proverbs 13:12 NKJV

*Sustain me as You promised, and I will live; do not let me be ashamed of my hope.*

Psalm 119:116 HCSB

*For I know the thoughts that I think toward you, says the Lord, thoughts of peace and not of evil, to give you a future and a hope. Then you will call upon Me and go and pray to Me, and I will listen to you.*

Jeremiah 29:11-12 NKJV

*Be of good courage, and He shall strengthen your heart, all you who hope in the Lord.*

Psalm 31:24 NKJV

## A Prayer

*Lord, I am only here on this earth for a brief while. But, You have offered me the priceless gift of eternal life through Your Son Jesus. I accept Your gift, Lord, with thanksgiving and praise. Let me share the good news of my salvation with those who need Your healing touch. Amen*

## Tasty Chicken Casserole

5 chicken breasts, cooked          1½ cups of sour cream
1 cup of bread crumbs               ½ cup melted butter
1 regular can cream of chicken soup

Remove skin and bones from chicken and chop. Mix chicken, soup and sour cream well and then place in a baking dish. Combine bread crumbs and melted butter in a bowl and toss lightly. Sprinkle the bread mixture over the chicken mixture and bake at 350°F for 25 minutes or until the dish is bubbling.

# Chapter 22

# God Protects

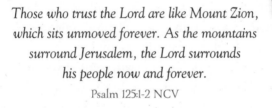

*Those who trust the Lord are like Mount Zion,*
*which sits unmoved forever. As the mountains*
*surround Jerusalem, the Lord surrounds*
*his people now and forever.*

Psalm 125:1-2 NCV

## *Today's Big Idea*

You are protected by God . . . now and always.
The only security that lasts is the security that flows
from the loving heart of God.

You have many responsibilities, inside the kitchen and out. As a busy woman, you know from first-hand experience that life is not always easy. But as a recipient of God's grace, you also know that you are protected by a loving Heavenly Father.

Have you ever faced challenges that seemed too big to handle? Have you ever faced big problems that, despite your best efforts, simply could not be solved? If so, you know how uncomfortable it is to feel helpless in the face of difficult circumstances. Thankfully, even when there's nowhere else to turn, you can turn your thoughts and prayers to God, and He will respond.

In times of trouble, God will comfort you; in times of sorrow, He will dry your tears. When you are troubled, or weak, or sorrowful, God is neither distant nor disinterested. To the contrary, God is always present and always vitally engaged in the events of your life. Reach out to Him, and build your future on the rock that cannot be shaken...trust in God and rely upon His provisions. He can provide everything you really need . . . and more.

## A Timely Tip

If you'd like infinite protection, there's only one place you can receive it: from an infinite God. So remember: when you live in the center of God's will, you will also be living in the center of God's protection.

## *More Ideas about God's Protection*

Our future may look fearfully intimidating, yet we can look up to the Engineer of the Universe, confident that nothing escapes His attention or slips out of the control of those strong hands.

Elisabeth Elliot

Worries carry responsibilities that belong to God, not to you. Worry does not enable us to escape evil; it makes us unfit to cope with it when it comes.

Corrie ten Boom

Only believe, don't fear. Our Master, Jesus, always watches over us, and no matter what the persecution, Jesus will surely overcome it.

Lottie Moon

God will never let you sink under your circumstances. He always provide a safety net and His love always encircles.

Barbara Johnson

The Rock of Ages is the great sheltering encirclement.

Oswald Chambers


A God wise enough to create me and the world I live in is wise enough to watch out for me.

Philip Yancey


We are never out of reach of Satan's devices, so we must never be without the whole armor of God.

Warren Wiersbe


As sure as God puts his children in the furnace, he will be in the furnace with them.

C. H. Spurgeon


The promises of God's Word sustain us in our suffering, and we know Jesus sympathizes and empathizes with us in our darkest hour.

Bill Bright

## More from God's Word

*Finally, my brethren, be strong in the Lord and in the power of His might. Put on the whole armor of God, that you may be able to stand against the wiles of the devil.*

Ephesians 6:10-11 NKJV

*The Lord your God in your midst, The Mighty One, will save; He will rejoice over you with gladness, He will quiet you with His love, He will rejoice over you with singing.*

Zephaniah 3:17 NKJV

*God is my shield, saving those whose hearts are true and right.*

Psalm 7:10 NLT

*But the Lord will be a refuge for His people.*

Joel 3:16 HCSB

*The Lord bless you and protect you; the Lord make His face shine on you, and be gracious to you.*

Numbers 6:24-25 HCSB

## A Prayer

*Lord, You are my Shepherd. You care for me; You comfort me; You watch over me; and You have saved me. I will praise You, Father, for Your glorious works, for Your protection, for Your love, and for Your Son. Amen*

## Marvelous Marshmallow Salad

| | |
|---|---|
| 1 package of cream cheese (6 oz.) | 2 tablespoon sugar |
| ½ cup of cherries (drained) | 1 tablespoon mayonnaise |
| 1 cup chopped nuts | 1 cup whipping cream |
| 4 cups marshmallows | 1 small can of crushed pineapples |

Combine the cream cheese, sugar, cherries, and mayonnaise in a large mixing bowl. Then, fold in the chopped nuts and whipping cream. Finally, add the marshmallows and pineapple. Chill before serving.

# Chapter 23

# He Is with You in the Kitchen . . . and Everywhere Else

*Draw near to God, and He will draw near to you.*

James 4:8 HCSB

### *Today's Big Idea*

God isn't far away—He's right here, right now.
And He's willing to talk to you right here, right now.

If you are a busy woman with more obligations than you have time to count, you know all too well that the demands of everyday life can, on occasion, seem overwhelming. Thankfully, even on the days when you feel overburdened, overworked, overstressed and underappreciated, God is trying to get His message through . . . your job is to listen.

Are you tired, discouraged or fearful? Be comforted because God is with you. Are you confused? Listen to the quiet voice of your Heavenly Father. Are you bitter? Talk with God and seek His guidance. In whatever condition you find yourself—whether you are happy or sad, victorious or vanquished, troubled or triumphant—carve out moments of silent solitude to celebrate God's gifts and to experience His presence.

The familiar words of Psalm 46:10 remind us to "Be still, and know that I am God." When we are still before the Creator, we encounter the awesome presence of our loving Heavenly Father, and we are comforted in the knowledge that God is not just near. He is here.

## A Timely Tip

Having trouble hearing God? If so, slow yourself down, tune out the distractions, and listen carefully. God has important things to say; your task is to be still and listen.

## *More Ideas about God's Presence*

God's presence is such a cleansing fire, confession and repentance are always there.

Anne Ortlund

What God promises is that He always, always comes. He always shows up. He always saves. He always rescues. His timing is not ours. His methods are usually unconventional. But what we can know, what we can settle in our soul, is that He is faithful to come when we call.

Angela Thomas

Through the death and broken body of Jesus Christ on the Cross, you and I have been given access to the presence of God when we approach Him by faith in prayer.

Anne Graham Lotz

The love of God is so vast, the power of his touch so invigorating, we could just stay in his presence for hours, soaking up his glory, basking in his blessings.

Debra Evans

If you want to hear God's voice clearly and you are uncertain, then remain in His presence until He changes that uncertainty. Often, much can happen during this waiting for the Lord. Sometimes, he changes pride into humility, doubt into faith and peace.

Corrie ten Boom

The Lord Jesus by His Holy Spirit is with me, and the knowledge of His presence dispels the darkness and allays any fears.

Bill Bright

Whatever we have done in the past, be it good or evil, great or small, is irrelevant to our stance before God today. It is only now that we are in the presence of God.

Brennan Manning

It's a crazy world and life speeds by at a blur, yet God is right in the middle of the craziness. And anywhere, at anytime, we may turn to Him, hear His voice, feel His hand, and catch the fragrance of heaven.

Joni Eareckson Tada

## *More from God's Word*

*You will seek Me and find Me when you search for Me with all your heart.*

Jeremiah 29:13 HCSB

*The Lord is near all who call out to Him, all who call out to Him with integrity. He fulfills the desires of those who fear Him; He hears their cry for help and saves them.*

Psalm 145:18-19 HCSB

*Surely goodness and mercy shall follow me all the days of my life: and I will dwell in the house of the Lord for ever.*

Psalm 23:6 KJV

*I am not alone, because the Father is with Me.*

John 16:32 HCSB

*Fear not, for I am with you; be not dismayed, for I am your God. I will strengthen you.*

Isaiah 41:10 NKJV

## A Prayer

*Dear Lord, You are with me always. Help me feel Your presence in every situation and every circumstance. Today, Dear God, let me feel You and acknowledge Your presence, Your love, and Your Son. Amen*

## Old-Fashioned Jam Cake

| | |
|---|---|
| 2 cups sugar | 2 cups buttermilk |
| 1 cup shortening | 3 eggs, beaten |
| 3 cups sifted flour | ¼ teaspoon salt |
| 1½ teaspoons baking soda | 1 teaspoon cinnamon |
| 1 teaspoon nutmeg | 1 teaspoon ground cloves |
| 1 teaspoon allspice | 1½ cups jam (your choice) |

Mix sugar with shortening; add eggs and blend. Sift remaining dry ingredients together. Add sugar and shortening mix to dry ingredients and gradually stir in buttermilk. Finally, stir in jam (but don't over-stir). Bake in greased and floured cake pan at 350° for 25 to 30 minutes or until cake tests done. When cool, you may wish to frost with an icing of your choice.

# Chapter 24

# Praise Him

*Praise the Lord, all nations! Glorify Him, all peoples!*
*For great is His faithful love to us;*
*the Lord's faithfulness endures forever. Hallelujah!*
Psalm 117 HCSB

## Today's Big Idea

God deserves your praise . . . and you deserve
the experience of praising Him.

When is the best time to praise God? In church? Before dinner is served? When we tuck little children into bed? None of the above. The best time to praise God is all day, every day, to the greatest extent we can, with thanksgiving in our hearts, and with a song on our lips.

Too many of us, even well-intentioned believers, tend to "compartmentalize" our waking hours into a few familiar categories: work, rest, play, family time, and worship. To do so is a mistake. Worship and praise should be woven into the fabric of everything we do; it should never be relegated to a weekly three-hour visit to church on Sunday morning.

The words by Fanny Crosby are familiar: "This is my story, this is my song, praising my Savior, all the day long." As believers who have been saved by the sacrifice of a risen Christ, we must do exactly as the song instructs: We must praise our Savior time and time again throughout the day. Worship and praise should be a part of everything we do. Otherwise, we quickly lose perspective as we fall prey to the demands of everyday life.

Theologian Wayne Oates once admitted, "Many of my prayers are made with my eyes open. You see, it seems I'm always praying about something, and it's not always convenient—or safe—to close my eyes." Dr. Oates understood that God always hears our prayers and that the relative position of our eyelids is of no concern to Him.

Do you sincerely desire to be a worthy servant of the One who has given you eternal love and eternal life? Then praise Him for who He is and for what He has done for you. And don't just praise Him on Sunday morning. Praise Him all day long, every day, for as long as you live . . . and then for all eternity.

## A Timely Tip

The appropriate moment to praise God is always this one.

## More Ideas about Praise

Words fail to express my love for this holy Book, my gratitude for its author, for His love and goodness. How shall I thank him for it?

Lottie Moon

A child of God should be a visible beatitude for joy and a living doxology for gratitude.

C. H. Spurgeon

Praise reestablishes the proper chain of command; we recognize that the King is on the throne and that he has saved his people.

Max Lucado

Nothing we do is more powerful or more life-changing than praising God.

Stormie Omartian

Praise is the highest occupation of any being.

Max Lucado

## More from God's Word

*But I will hope continually and will praise You more and more.*

Psalm 71:14 HCSB

*Therefore, through Him let us continually offer up to God a sacrifice of praise, that is, the fruit of our lips that confess His name.*

Hebrews 13:15 HCSB

*So that at the name of Jesus every knee should bow—of those who are in heaven and on earth and under the earth—and every tongue should confess that Jesus Christ is Lord, to the glory of God the Father.*

Philippians 2:10-11 HCSB

*Enter into his gates with thanksgiving, and into his courts with praise: be thankful unto him, and bless his name. For the LORD is good; his mercy is everlasting; and his truth endureth to all generations.*

Psalm 100:4-5 KJV

## A Prayer

*Dear Lord, make me a woman who gives constant praise to You. And, let me share the joyous news of Jesus Christ with a world that needs His transformation and His salvation. Amen*

## Gluten-free Cranberry Corn Muffins

1 ½ cups of corn flour            ½ cup of corn meal
1 teaspoon baking powder      1 teaspoon baking soda
1 cup of dried cranberries (or substitute raisins)
2 eggs                        ¼ cup melted butter or olive oil
1 cup of vanilla coconut milk

For gluten-free recipe substitute vanilla coconut milk for
1 regular cup milk, 1/4 cup honey, 1 teaspoon of gluten-free vanilla

Mix all dry ingredients in a large bowl. In a small bowl beat eggs, coconut milk, melted butter or oil, then add dried cranberries. Add wet mixture gradually to dry mixture and stir until smooth. Put into greased muffin tins and bake at 350° for about 15 minutes or until top and bottom of muffins are brown.

# Chapter 25

# Obey Him

*You must follow the Lord your God and fear Him.*
*You must keep His commands and listen to His voice;*
*you must worship Him and remain faithful to Him.*

Deuteronomy 13:4 HCSB

## Today's Big Idea

Because God is just, He rewards good behavior
just as surely as He punishes sin. Obedience earns
God's pleasure; disobedience doesn't.

At one time or another, we all face a similar temptation—the temptation to follow some of God's rules and disregard others. But if we're wise, we won't pick and choose among the Bible's commandments . . . we'll do our best to obey them all, not just the ones that are easy or convenient. When we do, we are most certainly blessed by our loving, heavenly Father.

Today, Mom, whether you're at home, at work, or anyplace in between, take every step of your journey with God as your traveling companion. Read His Word and take it seriously. Support only those activities that further your own spiritual growth. Be a positive example to your children, to your friends, to your neighbors, and to your community. Then, prepare yourself for the countless blessings God has promised to all those who trust—and obey—Him completely.

## A Timely Tip

If your family members don't learn obedience between the four walls of your home, they probably won't learn it anywhere else.

## More Ideas about Obedience

Rejoicing is a matter of obedience to God—an obedience that will start you on the road to peace and contentment.

Kay Arthur

God asked both Noah and Joshua to do something unusual and difficult. They did it, and their obedience brought them deliverance.

Mary Morrison Suggs

Obedience goes before our hearts and carries them where they would not normally go.

Paula Rinehart

Obey God one step at a time, then the next step will come into view.

Catherine Marshall

I know the power obedience has for making things easy which seem impossible.

St. Teresa of Avila

The pathway of obedience can sometimes be difficult, but it always leads to a strengthening of our inner woman.

Vonette Bright

God is God. Because He is God, He is worthy of my trust and obedience. I will find rest nowhere but in His holy will, a will that is unspeakably beyond my largest notions of what He is up to.

Elisabeth Elliot

God is not hard to please. He does not expect us to be absolutely perfect. He just expects us to keep moving toward Him and believing in Him, letting Him work with us to bring us into conformity to His will and ways.

Joyce Meyer

A wholehearted love for God looks to Him through His Word and prayer, always watching and waiting, ever ready to do all that He says, prepared to act on His expressed desires.

Elizabeth George

## *More from God's Word*

*Therefore, get your minds ready for action, being self-disciplined, and set your hope completely on the grace to be brought to you at the revelation of Jesus Christ. As obedient children, do not be conformed to the desires of your former ignorance but, as the One who called you is holy, you also are to be holy in all your conduct.*

1 Peter 1:13-15 HCSB

*Who is wise and understanding among you? He should show his works by good conduct with wisdom's gentleness.*

James 3:13 HCSB

*But whoever keeps His word, truly the love of God is perfected in him. By this we know that we are in Him. He who says he abides in Him ought himself also to walk just as He walked.*

1 John 2:5-6 NKJV

*Because the eyes of the Lord are on the righteous and His ears are open to their request. But the face of the Lord is against those who do evil.*

1 Peter 3:12 HCSB

## A Prayer

*Dear Lord, make me a woman who is obedient to Your Word. Let me live according to Your commandments. Direct my path far from the temptations and distractions of this world. And, let me discover Your will and follow it, Lord, this day and always. Amen*

## Homemade Potato Soup

6 potatoes, peeled and diced

1 large onion

3 tablespoon all-purpose flour

2 cubes chicken bouillon

2 carrots, diced

½ teaspoon ground black pepper

3 cups of milk

¼ cup butter or margarine

3 cups water

¼ teaspoon dried thyme

1 tablespoon dried parsley

Cook onion in butter until tender. In a separate stockpot, bring the diced potatoes, carrots, water, and chicken bouillon to a boil. Simmer about 10 minutes or until tender. Add ground black pepper. Add the flour to the cooked onions in order to make a paste. Stir in milk. Cook over low heat stirring constantly until warmed throughout. Add the potato and carrot mixture. Stir in the parsley and thyme and heat. Serve and enjoy!

# Chapter 26

# Beyond Worry

*So do not worry, saying, "What shall we eat?" or
"What shall we drink?" or "What shall we wear?"
For the pagans run after all these things, and your heavenly
Father knows that you need them. But seek first his kingdom
and his righteousness, and all these things will be given to you
as well. Therefore do not worry about tomorrow,
for tomorrow will worry about itself.
Each day has enough trouble of its own.*

Matthew 6:31-34 NIV

### Today's Big Idea

You have worries, but God has solutions.
Your challenge is to trust Him to solve
the problems that you can't.

I f you are like most women, it is simply a fact of life: from time to time, you worry. You worry about children, about health, about finances, about safety, and about countless other challenges of life, some great and some small. Where is the best place to take your worries? Take them to God. Take your troubles to Him, and your fears, and your sorrows.

Barbara Johnson correctly observed, "Worry is the senseless process of cluttering up tomorrow's opportunities with leftover problems from today." So if you'd like to make the most out of this day (and every one hereafter), turn your worries over to a Power greater than yourself . . . and spend your valuable time and energy solving the problems you can fix . . . while trusting God to do the rest.

## *A Timely Tip*

Work hard, pray harder, and if you have any worries, take them to God—and leave them there.

## *More Ideas about Worry*

The secret of Christian quietness is not indifference, but the knowledge that God is my Father, He loves me, and that I shall never think of anything that He will forget. Then, worry becomes an impossibility.

Oswald Chambers

God is bigger than your problems. Whatever worries press upon you today, put them in God's hands and leave them there.

Billy Graham

We are not called to be burden-bearers, but cross-bearers and light-bearers. We must cast our burdens on the Lord.

Corrie ten Boom

This life of faith, then, consists in just this—being a child in the Father's house. Let the ways of childish confidence and freedom from care, which so please you and win your heart when you observe your own little ones, teach you what you should be in your attitude toward God.

Hannah Whitall Smith

Pray, and let God worry.

Martin Luther

Today is mine. Tomorrow is none of my business. If I peer anxiously into the fog of the future, I will strain my spiritual eyes so that I will not see clearly what is required of me now.

Elisabeth Elliott

Worry and anxiety are sand in the machinery of life; faith is the oil.

E. Stanley Jones

Today is the tomorrow we worried about yesterday.

Dennis Swanberg

Worries carry responsibilities that belong to God, not to you. Worry does not enable us to escape evil; it makes us unfit to cope with it when it comes.

Corrie ten Boom

## *More from God's Word*

*Come to Me, all you who labor and are heavy laden, and I will give you rest. Take My yoke upon you and learn from Me, for I am gentle and lowly in heart, and you will find rest for your souls. For My yoke is easy and My burden is light.*

Matthew 11:28-30 NKJV

*An anxious heart weighs a man down....*

Proverbs 12:25 NIV

*Don't fret or worry. Instead of worrying, pray. Let petitions and praises shape your worries into prayers, letting God know your concerns. Before you know it, a sense of God's wholeness, everything coming together for good, will come and settle you down. It's wonderful what happens when Christ displaces worry at the center of your life.*

Philippians 4:6-7 MSG

*Those who trust in the Lord are like Mount Zion. It cannot be shaken; it remains forever.*

Psalm 125:1 HCSB

## A Prayer

*Dear Lord, wherever I find myself, let me celebrate more and worry less. When my faith begins to waver, help me to trust You more. Then, with praise on my lips and the love of Your Son in my heart, let me live courageously, faithfully, prayerfully, and thankfully this day and every day. Amen*

## Spicy Mexican Tomato-Vegetable Soup

| | |
|---|---|
| Approx. ½ liter tomato sauce | 2 large onions |
| 1 can of sweet corn | ¼ cup vegetable or olive oil |
| Salt (to taste) | Sugar (to taste) |
| 2 red peppers | 2 tomatoes |
| plus a mixture of your favorite vegetables | |

Chop onions and fry lightly in a large sauce pan with a bit of oil. Add vegetables in their logical order. Add salt, tomato sauce, and corn, then add sugar. Serve with tortilla chips and enjoy!

# Chapter 27

# He Has a Plan

*We know that all things work together for the good
of those who love God: those who are called
according to His purpose.*

Romans 8:28 HCSB

## Today's Big Idea

God has a plan for the world, for your family,
and for you. When you discover His plan for your life—
and when you follow in the footsteps of His Son—
you will be rewarded. The place where God is leading
you is the place where you must go.

Whether you realize it or not, Mom, God is busily at work at your house. He has things He wants your family to do, and He has people He wants your family to help. Your assignment, should you choose to accept it, is to seek the will of God and to follow it, wherever it may lead.

Sometimes, God's plans are obvious to us—but at other times, we may be genuinely puzzled about the direction our lives should take. In either case, we should consult our heavenly Father on a regular (spelled d-a-i-l-y) basis. And we should also consult trusted friends and family members who can help us discern God's will. When we do these things, God will make Himself known, and He will signify His approval by the blessings He bestows upon us and our loved ones.

## A Timely Tip

God has a wonderful plan for your life. And the time to start looking for that plan—and living it—is now. Discovering God's plan begins with prayer, but it doesn't end there. You've also got to work at it.

## More Ideas about God's Plan

With God, it's never "Plan B" or "second best." It's always "Plan A." And, if we let Him, He'll make something beautiful of our lives.

Gloria Gaither

God has a plan for the life of every Christian. Every circumstance, every turn of destiny, all things work together for your good and for His glory.

Billy Graham

God wants us to serve Him with a willing spirit, one that would choose no other way.

Beth Moore

I don't doubt that the Holy Spirit guides your decisions from within when you make them with the intention of pleasing God. The error would be to think that He speaks only within, whereas in reality He speaks also through Scripture, the Church, Christian friends, and books.

C. S. Lewis

God has a course mapped out for your life, and all the inadequacies in the world will not change His mind. He will be with you every step of the way. And though it may take time, He has a celebration planned for when you cross over the "Red Seas" of your life.

Charles Swindoll

The Lord never makes a mistake. One day, when we are in heaven, I'm sure we shall see the answers to all the whys. My, how often I have asked, "Why?" In heaven, we shall see God's side of the embroidery.

Corrie ten Boom

If you believe in a God who controls the big things, you have to believe in a God who controls the little things. It is we, of course, to whom things look "little" or "big."

Elisabeth Elliot

Ours is an intentional God, brimming over with motive and mission. He never does things capriciously or decides with the flip of a coin.

Joni Eareckson Tada

## *More from God's Word*

*But as it is written: What no eye has seen and no ear has heard, and what has never come into a man's heart, is what God has prepared for those who love Him.*

1 Corinthians 2:9 HCSB

*In Him we were also made His inheritance, predestined according to the purpose of the One who works out everything in agreement with the decision of His will.*

Ephesians 1:11 HCSB

*Yet Lord, You are our Father; we are the clay, and You are our potter; we all are the work of Your hands.*

Isaiah 64:8 HCSB

*The Lord is gracious and compassionate, slow to anger and great in faithful love. The Lord is good to everyone; His compassion [rests] on all He has made.*

Psalm 145:8-9 HCSB

## A Prayer

*Dear Lord, You have a plan for me and a plan for this world. Let me trust Your will, and let me discover Your plan for my life so that I can become the person You want me to become. Amen*

## Can't-Miss Old-Fashioned Cobbler

1 cup fresh fruit (apples, or peaches, or cherries, etc.)
½ cup (1 stick) of butter                1 cup milk
1 cup self-rising flour                  1 cup sugar
1 teaspoon baking powder

Preheat oven to 350°. Place the butter in a 9½" x 12" deep baking dish. Put dish in oven to melt butter while preparing other ingredients. If butter is unsalted, add a touch of salt to the pan as well. Add flour and sugar to a bowl and sift together lightly. Create a "well" in the center of the mixture and pour milk into the well. Then, mix together with a wire whisk until smooth. Remove pan from oven. Pour batter into dish on top of melted butter. Do not stir. Spoon the fresh fruit out evenly across the top. Do not stir. Place cobbler in oven and bake uncovered until golden brown.

# Chapter 28

# Using Your Talents

*According to the grace given to us, we have different gifts:*
*If prophecy, use it according to the standard of faith;*
*if service, in service; if teaching, in teaching; if exhorting,*
*in exhortation; giving, with generosity; leading,*
*with diligence; showing mercy, with cheerfulness.*

Romans 12:6-8 HCSB

## *Today's Big Idea*

God has given you a unique array of talents and
opportunities. The rest is up to you.

You possess an assortment of talents, both inside the kitchen and outside it. God has given you an array of gifts, and He has given you unique opportunities to share those gifts with the world. Your Creator intends for you to use your talents for the glory of His kingdom in the service of His children. Will you honor Him by sharing His gifts? And, will you share His gifts humbly and lovingly? Hopefully you will.

The old saying is both familiar and true: "What you are is God's gift to you; what you become is your gift to God." As a woman who has been touched by the transforming love of Jesus Christ, your obligation is clear: You must strive to make the most of your own God-given talents, and you must encourage your family and friends to do likewise.

Today, make this promise to yourself and to God: Promise to use your talents to minister to your family, to your friends, and to the world. And remember: The best way to say "Thank You" for God's gifts is to use them.

## A Timely Tip

It's both stressful and futile to squander God's blessings. You possess a unique set of talents. These gifts are from the Creator—use them while you can.

## *More Ideas about Talents*

God has given you special talents—now it's your turn to give them back to God.

*Marie T. Freeman*

Employ whatever God has entrusted you with, in doing good, all possible good, in every possible kind and degree.

*John Wesley*

If you want to reach your potential, you need to add a strong work ethic to your talent.

*John Maxwell*

Not everyone possesses boundless energy or a conspicuous talent. We are not equally blessed with great intellect or physical beauty or emotional strength. But we have all been given the same ability to be faithful.

*Gigi Graham Tchividjian*

You are the only person on earth who can use your ability.

*Zig Ziglar*

God often reveals His direction for our lives through the way He made us…with a certain personality and unique skills.

Bill Hybels

You are a unique blend of talents, skills, and gifts, which makes you an indispensable member of the body of Christ.

Charles Stanley

In the great orchestra we call life, you have an instrument and a song, and you owe it to God to play them both sublimely.

Max Lucado

If you want to reach your potential, you need to add a strong work ethic to your talent.

John Maxwell

## *More from God's Word*

*His master said to him, "Well done, good and faithful slave! You were faithful over a few things; I will put you in charge of many things. Enter your master's joy!"*

Matthew 25:21 HCSB

*Every good gift and every perfect gift is from above, and cometh down from the Father of lights.*

James 1:17 KJV

*Do not neglect the gift that is in you.*

1 Timothy 4:14 HCSB

*I remind you to keep ablaze the gift of God that is in you.*

2 Timothy 1:6 HCSB

*Whatever you do, do it enthusiastically, as something done for the Lord and not for men.*

Colossians 3:23 HCSB

### A Prayer

*Lord, You have given all of us talents, and I am no exception. You have blessed me with a gift—let me discover it, nurture it, and use it for the glory of Your Kingdom. I will share my gifts with the world, and I will praise to You, the Giver of all things good. Amen*

## Scrumptious Snickerdoodle Cookies

2 ¾ cups all-purpose flour          ¼ teaspoon salt
1 teaspoon baking soda          2 teaspoons cream of tartar
1 ½ cups white sugar          1 cup soft shortening
2 eggs, beaten

Heat oven to 400°. Mix ingredients, and bake for 10 minutes or until crisp and light brown. Sprinkle generously with cinnamon while hot.

# Chapter 29

# The Joys of Generosity

*So let each one give as he purposes in his heart,*
*not grudgingly or of necessity; for God loves a cheerful giver.*
2 Corinthians 9:7 NKJV

### Today's Big Idea

God has given so much to you,
and He wants you
to share His gifts with others.

The thread of generosity is woven—completely and inextricably—into the very fabric of Christ's teachings. As He sent His disciples out to heal the sick and spread God's message of salvation, Jesus offered this guiding principle: "Freely you have received, freely give" (Matthew 10:8 NIV). The principle still applies. If we are to be disciples of Christ, we must give freely of our time, our possessions, and our love.

Lisa Whelchel spoke for Christian women everywhere when she observed, "The Lord has abundantly blessed me all of my life. I'm not trying to pay Him back for all of His wonderful gifts; I just realize that He gave them to me to give away." All of us have been blessed, and all of us are called to share those blessings without reservation.

Today, make this pledge and keep it: Be a cheerful, generous, courageous giver. The world needs your help, and you need the spiritual rewards that will be yours when you share your possessions, your talents, and your time.

## A Timely Tip

Would you like to be a little happier? Try sharing a few more of the blessings that God has bestowed upon you. In other words, if you want to be happy, be generous. And if you want to be unhappy, be greedy.

## *More Ideas about Generosity*

We are never more like God than when we give.

Charles Swindoll

The measure of a life, after all, is not its duration but its donation.

Corrie ten Boom

The happiest and most joyful people are those who give money and serve.

Dave Ramsey

Abundant living means abundant giving.

E. Stanley Jones

The mark of a Christian is that he will walk the second mile and turn the other cheek. A wise man or woman gives the extra effort, all for the glory of the Lord Jesus Christ.

John Maxwell

Here lies the tremendous mystery—that God should be all-powerful, yet refuse to coerce. He summons us to cooperation. We are honored in being given the opportunity to participate in His good deeds. Remember how He asked for help in performing His miracles: Fill the water pots, stretch out your hand, distribute the loaves.

Elisabeth Elliot

God does not need our money. But, you and I need the experience of giving it.

James Dobson

What is your focus today? Joy comes when it is Jesus first, others second . . . then you.

Kay Arthur

When somebody needs a helping hand, he doesn't need it tomorrow or the next day. He needs it now, and that's exactly when you should offer to help. Good deeds, if they are really good, happen sooner rather than later.

Marie T. Freeman

## More from God's Word

*Dear friend, you are showing your faith by whatever you do for the brothers, and this you are doing for strangers.*

3 John 1:5 HCSB

*In every way I've shown you that by laboring like this, it is necessary to help the weak and to keep in mind the words of the Lord Jesus, for He said, "It is more blessed to give than to receive."*

Acts 20:35 HCSB

*If a brother or sister is without clothes and lacks daily food, and one of you says to them, "Go in peace, keep warm, and eat well," but you don't give them what the body needs, what good is it?*

James 2:15–16 HCSB

*The one who has two shirts must share with someone who has none, and the one who has food must do the same.*

Luke 3:11 HCSB

## A Prayer

*Lord, You have been so generous with me; let me be generous with others. Help me to give generously of my time and my possessions as I care for those in need. And, make me a humble giver, Lord, so that all the glory and the praise might be Yours. Amen*

## Amazing Ambrosia Fruit Salad

2 (11 oz.) cans mandarin orange segments, drained
2 (15 oz.) cans fruit cocktail, drained
2 cups flaked coconut
2 cups miniature marshmallows
1 (8 oz.) container of whipped cream or Cool Whip
1 (16 oz.) container sour cream
1 jar maraschino cherries, drained

Mix the mandarin oranges, fruit cocktail, and coconut in a large bowl. Fold in the whipped cream and marshmallows. Chill for at least an hour. Stir again before serving.

# Chapter 30

# God's Recipe for Eternal Life

*For God so loved the world that He gave*
*His only begotten Son, that whoever believes in Him*
*should not perish but have everlasting life.*

John 3:16 NKJV

## Today's Big Idea

God offers you life abundant and life eternal.
Accept His gift today.

Eternal life is not an event that begins when you die. Eternal life begins when you invite Jesus into your heart right here on earth. So it's important to remember that God's plans for you are not limited to the ups and downs of everyday life. If you've allowed Jesus to reign over your heart, you've already begun your eternal journey.

As mere mortals, our vision for the future, like our lives here on earth, is limited. God's vision is not burdened by such limitations: His plans extend throughout all eternity.

Let us praise the Creator for His priceless gift, and let us share the Good News with all who cross our paths. We return our Father's love by accepting His grace and by sharing His message and His love. When we do, we are blessed here on earth and throughout all eternity.

## A Timely Tip

God has created heaven and given you a way to get there. The rest is up to you. Make sure your family members know the way.

## *More Ideas about Eternal Life*

Your choice to either receive or reject the Lord Jesus Christ will determine where you spend eternity.

Anne Graham Lotz

If you are a believer, your judgment will not determine your eternal destiny. Christ's finished work on Calvary was applied to you the moment you accepted Christ as Savior.

Beth Moore

I can still hardly believe it. I, with shriveled, bent fingers, atrophied muscles, gnarled knees, and no feeling from the shoulders down, will one day have a new body— light, bright and clothed in righteousness—powerful and dazzling.

Joni Eareckson Tada

Slowly and surely, we learn the great secret of life, which is to know God.

Oswald Chambers

God has promised us abundance, peace, and eternal life. These treasures are ours for the asking; all we must do is claim them. One of the great mysteries of life is why on earth do so many of us wait so very long to lay claim to God's gifts?

*Marie T. Freeman*

The damage done to us on this earth will never find its way into that safe city. We can relax, we can rest, and though some of us can hardly imagine it, we can prepare to feel safe and secure for all of eternity.

*Bill Hybels*

Teach us to set our hopes on heaven, to hold firmly to the promise of eternal life, so that we can withstand the struggles and storms of this world.

*Max Lucado*

## *More from God's Word*

*And this is the testimony: God has given us eternal life, and this life is in His Son. The one who has the Son has life. The one who doesn't have the Son of God does not have life. I have written these things to you who believe in the name of the Son of God, so that you may know that you have eternal life.*

1 John 5:11-13 HCSB

*We do not want you to be uninformed, brothers, concerning those who are asleep, so that you will not grieve like the rest, who have no hope. Since we believe that Jesus died and rose again, in the same way God will bring with Him those who have fallen asleep through Jesus.*

1 Thessalonians 4:13-14 HCSB

*Jesus said to her, "I am the resurrection and the life. The one who believes in Me, even if he dies, will live. Everyone who lives and believes in Me will never die—ever. Do you believe this?"*

John 11:25-26 HCSB

## A Prayer

*Lord, You have given me the priceless gift of eternal life through Your Son Jesus. Keep the hope of heaven fresh in my heart. While I am in this world, help me to pass through it with faith in my heart and praise on my lips for You. Amen*

## Old-Fashioned Candied Sweet Potatoes

6 large sweet potatoes boiled, peeled, and sliced
1 cup brown sugar            ¼ cup butter (melted)
½ teaspoon salt              ½ cup pecans

Place potatoes in greased casserole; combine remaining ingredients, and pour over potatoes. Bake at 350° for 45 minutes, basting occasionally. Makes 8 servings.

# More from God's Word About . . .

## Acceptance

A man's heart plans his way, but the Lord determines his steps.

Proverbs 16:9 HCSB

For everything created by God is good, and nothing should be rejected if it is received with thanksgiving.

1 Timothy 4:4 HCSB

Should we accept only good from God and not adversity?

Job 2:10 HCSB

Come to terms with God and be at peace; in this way good will come to you.

Job 22:21 HCSB

Sheathe your sword! Should I not drink the cup that the Father has given Me?

John 18:11 HCSB

## Anger

*Don't let your spirit rush to be angry, for anger abides in the heart of fools.*

*Ecclesiastes 7:9 HCSB*

*My dearly loved brothers, understand this: everyone must be quick to hear, slow to speak, and slow to anger, for man's anger does not accomplish God's righteousness.*

*James 1:19-20 HCSB*

*A fool's displeasure is known at once, but whoever ignores an insult is sensible.*

*Proverbs 12:16 HCSB*

*All bitterness, anger and wrath, insult and slander must be removed from you, along with all wickedness. And be kind and compassionate to one another, forgiving one another, just as God also forgave you in Christ.*

*Ephesians 4:31-32 HCSB*

*A gentle answer turns away anger, but a harsh word stirs up wrath.*

*Proverbs 15:1 HCSB*

## Behavior

*Don't be deceived: God is not mocked. For whatever a man sows he will also reap, because the one who sows to his flesh will reap corruption from the flesh, but the one who sows to the Spirit will reap eternal life from the Spirit.*

Galatians 6:7-8 HCSB

*Therefore, get your minds ready for action, being self-disciplined, and set your hope completely on the grace to be brought to you at the revelation of Jesus Christ. As obedient children, do not be conformed to the desires of your former ignorance but, as the One who called you is holy, you also are to be holy in all your conduct.*

1 Peter 1:13-15 HCSB

*For this very reason, make every effort to supplement your faith with goodness, goodness with knowledge, knowledge with self-control, self-control with endurance, endurance with godliness.*

2 Peter 1:5-6 HCSB

*Therefore as you have received Christ Jesus the Lord, walk in Him.*

Colossians 2:6 HCSB

## *Bitterness*

*All bitterness, anger and wrath, insult and slander must be removed from you, along with all wickedness. And be kind and compassionate to one another, forgiving one another, just as God also forgave you in Christ.*

*Ephesians 4:31-32 HCSB*

*But if you harbor bitter envy and selfish ambition in your hearts, do not boast about it or deny the truth. Such "wisdom" does not come down from heaven but is earthly, unspiritual, of the devil. For where you have envy and selfish ambition, there you find disorder and every evil practice.*

*James 3:14-16 NIV*

*The heart knows its own bitterness, and a stranger does not share its joy.*

*Proverbs 14:10 NKJV*

*Don't insist on getting even; that's not for you to do. "I'll do the judging," says God. "I'll take care of it."*

*Romans 12:19 MSG*

*See to it that no one repays evil for evil to anyone, but always pursue what is good for one another and for all.*

*1 Thessalonians 5:15 HCSB*

## Blessings

*You will show me the path of life; in Your presence is fullness of joy; at Your right hand are pleasures forevermore.*

*Psalm 16:11 NKJV*

*I will make them and the area around My hill a blessing: I will send down showers in their season—showers of blessing.*

*Ezekiel 34:26 HCSB*

*Obey My voice, and I will be your God, and you shall be my people. And walk in all the ways that I have commanded you, that it may be well with you.*

*Jeremiah 7:23 NKJV*

*The Lord bless you and keep you; the Lord make His face shine upon you, and be gracious to you.*

*Numbers 6:24-25 NKJV*

*Blessed is a man who endures trials, because when he passes the test he will receive the crown of life that He has promised to those who love Him.*

*James 1:12 HCSB*

## *Conscience*

*Now the goal of our instruction is love from a pure heart, a good conscience, and a sincere faith.*

1 Timothy 1:5 HCSB

*If then you were raised with Christ, seek those things which are above, where Christ is, sitting at the right hand of God. Set your mind on things above, not on things on the earth.*

Colossians 3:1-2 NKJV

*And do not be conformed to this world, but be transformed by the renewing of your mind, that you may prove what is that good and acceptable and perfect will of God.*

Romans 12:2 NKJV

*For indeed, the kingdom of God is within you.*

Luke 17:21 NKJV

*I always do my best to have a clear conscience toward God and men.*

Acts 24:16 HCSB

## Courage

Be strong and courageous, and do the work. Don't be afraid or discouraged, for the Lord God, my God, is with you. He won't leave you or forsake you.

1 Chronicles 28:20 HCSB


For God has not given us a spirit of fearfulness, but one of power, love, and sound judgment.

2 Timothy 1:7 HCSB


Be alert, stand firm in the faith, be brave and strong.

1 Corinthians 16:13 HCSB


Haven't I commanded you: be strong and courageous? Do not be afraid or discouraged, for the Lord your God is with you wherever you go.

Joshua 1:9 HCSB


But when Jesus heard it, He answered him, "Don't be afraid. Only believe."

Luke 8:50 HCSB

## Discipleship

"Follow Me," Jesus told them, "and I will make you into fishers of men!" Immediately they left their nets and followed Him.

*Mark 1:17-18 HCSB*

You did not choose Me, but I chose you. I appointed you that you should go out and produce fruit, and that your fruit should remain, so that whatever you ask the Father in My name, He will give you.

*John 15:16 HCSB*

But whoever keeps His word, truly in him the love of God is perfected. This is how we know we are in Him: the one who says he remains in Him should walk just as He walked.

*1 John 2:5-6 HCSB*

The one who loves his life will lose it, and the one who hates his life in this world will keep it for eternal life. If anyone serves Me, he must follow Me. Where I am, there My servant also will be. If anyone serves Me, the Father will honor him.

*John 12:25-26 HCSB*

## *Doubts*

*If you don't know what you're doing, pray to the Father. He loves to help. You'll get his help, and won't be condescended to when you ask for it. Ask boldly, believingly, without a second thought. People who "worry their prayers" are like wind-whipped waves. Don't think you're going to get anything from the Master that way, adrift at sea, keeping all your options open.*

*James 1:5-8 MSG*

*Purify your hearts, ye double-minded.*

*James 4:8 KJV*

*Immediately the father of the child cried out and said with tears, "Lord, I believe; help my unbelief!"*

*Mark 9:24 NKJV*

*So He said, "Come." And when Peter had come down out of the boat, he walked on the water to go to Jesus. But when he saw that the wind was boisterous, he was afraid; and beginning to sink he cried out, saying, "Lord, save me!" And immediately Jesus stretched out His hand and caught him, and said to him, "O you of little faith, why did you doubt?" And when they got into the boat, the wind ceased.*

*Matthew 14:29-32 NKJV*

## *Forgiveness*

*Then Jesus said, "Father, forgive them, for they do not know what they do." And they divided His garments and cast lots.*

Luke 23:34 NKJV

*When they persisted in questioning Him, He stood up and said to them, "The one without sin among you should be the first to throw a stone at her."*

John 8:7 HCSB

*And forgive us our sins, for we ourselves also forgive everyone in debt to us.*

Luke 11:4 HCSB

*Do not judge, and you will not be judged. Do not condemn, and you will not be condemned. Forgive, and you will be forgiven.*

Luke 6:37 HCSB

*And whenever you stand praying, if you have anything against anyone, forgive him, so that your Father in heaven may also forgive you your wrongdoing.*

Mark 11:25 HCSB

## Friends

*I give thanks to my God for every remembrance of you.*

Philippians 1:3 HCSB

*Beloved, if God so loved us, we also ought to love one another.*

1 John 4:11 NKJV

*A friend loves at all times, and a brother is born for a difficult time.*

Proverbs 17:17 HCSB

*Iron sharpens iron, and one man sharpens another.*

Proverbs 27:17 HCSB

*Finally, all of you be of one mind, having compassion for one another; love as brothers, be tenderhearted, be courteous.*

1 Peter 3:8 NKJV

## Miracles

*Looking at them, Jesus said, "With men it is impossible, but not with God, because all things are possible with God."*

Mark 10:27 HCSB

*I assure you: The one who believes in Me will also do the works that I do. And he will do even greater works than these, because I am going to the Father.*

John 14:12 HCSB

*But as it is written: "Eye has not seen, nor ear heard, nor have entered into the heart of man the things which God has prepared for those who love Him."*

1 Corinthians 2:9 NKJV

*For nothing will be impossible with God.*

Luke 1:37 HCSB

*You are the God who works wonders; You revealed Your strength among the peoples.*

Psalm 77:14 HCSB

## Sabbath

*Six days shall work be done, but the seventh day is a Sabbath of solemn rest, a holy convocation. You shall do no work on it; it is the Sabbath of the Lord in all your dwellings.*

Leviticus 23:3 NKJV

*Then He told them, "The Sabbath was made for man, and not man for the Sabbath."*

Mark 2:27 HCSB

*For the Son of Man is the Lord of the Sabbath.*

Matthew 12:8 NIV

*What's important in all this is that if you keep a holy day, keep it for God's sake; if you eat meat, eat it to the glory of God and thank God for prime rib; if you're a vegetarian, eat vegetables to the glory of God and thank God for broccoli.*

Romans 14:6 MSG

*Worship the Lord with gladness. Come before him, singing with joy. Acknowledge that the Lord is God! He made us, and we are his. We are his people, the sheep of his pasture.*

Psalm 100:2-3 NLT

## *Values*

*Sow righteousness for yourselves and reap faithful love; break up your untilled ground. It is time to seek the Lord until He comes and sends righteousness on you like the rain.*

Hosea 10:12 HCSB


*Teach me, O Lord, the way of Your statutes, and I shall keep it to the end.*

Psalm 119:33 NKJV


*For it is God who is working among you both the willing and the working for His good purpose.*

Philippians 2:13 HCSB


*Do what is right and good in the Lord's sight, so that you may prosper and so that you may enter and possess the good land the Lord your God swore to [give] your fathers.*

Deuteronomy 6:18 HCSB


*You will know the truth, and the truth will set you free.*

John 8:32 HCSB

# Index of Recipes